FATAL JOURNEY
The Murder of Trevor O'Keeffe

JANE KELLY is a television executive producer, director and broadcaster. A former BBC producer, she has written, produced and directed programmes over the last fifteen years for the BBC, RTÉ, UTV, TG4, Granada Television and Living TV.

She spent time at the BBC's New York Bureau where she produced news and current affairs. In 2005 she set up her own independent production company with her husband and award-winning producer, Philip McGovern, who has made two documentaries about Trevor O'Keeffe for RTÉ.

FATAL JOURNEY

The Murder of Trevor O'Keeffe

EROLINE O'KEEFFE

With Jane Kelly

THE O'BRIEN PRESS
DUBLIN

First published 2006 by The O'Brien Press Ltd,
12 Terenure Road East, Rathgar, Dublin 6, Ireland.
Tel: +353 1 4923333; Fax: +353 1 4922777
E-mail: books@obrien.ie
Website: www.obrien.ie

ISBN-10: 0-86278-913-3
ISBN-13: 978-0-86278-913-8

British Library Cataloguing-in-Publication Data
O'Keeffe, Eroline
Fatal journey : the murder of Trevor O'Keeffe
1. O'Keeffe, Trevor - Death and burial
2. Chanal, Pierre - Trials, litigation, etc.
3. Serial murderers - France
4. Serial murder investigation - France
I. Title II. Kelly, Jane
364.1'523'092

1 2 3 4 5 6 7 8 9 10
06 07 08 09 10

Editing, typesetting, layout and design: The O'Brien Press Ltd
Printing: Nørhaven Paperback A/S

Picture Credits: Front cover and First Section, pages 1, 2, 3, 4, 5 & 6, Eroline
O'Keeffe; p8 (top) Gamma, Camera Press London; p8 (bottom), Noeleen Slattery.
Second section, p1 (top left), Noeleen Slattery; (top right & bottom) Eroline
O'Keeffe; p2 & 3, Gamma, Camera Press London; p4, Noeleen Slattery; p5, Gamma,
Camera Press London; p6, Eroline O'Keeffe; p7 & p8 (top), Gamma, Camera Press
London; (bottom), Eroline O'Keeffe.

To my dearly beloved son, Trevor

Acknowledgements

Since my son, Trevor, was murdered in 1987, I have been on a journey I never expected to take. My life and the lives of my children changed forever. All I or my family ever wanted was justice for Trevor: to find his killer and have him brought to court and punished for what he did. Despite all the setbacks I suffered at the hands of the French justice system, I feel I have been privileged in the people I met along the way who gave me their time, expert advice and, ultimately, their friendship.

I would like to thank Joëlle Charuel for her honesty and ingenuity, without which we would never have known where Trevor's belongings ended up nor how the find tied a crucial location into the case.

I thank Éamon Ó Ciosáin for the last ten years of help, translations from French to English and excellent advice. He has made my journey clearer with his guidance.

I thank Dominique Rizet for his practical assistance over the years at various courts, his expert guidance and friendship and for being a good and honest journalist. I thank him, too, for introducing me to Eric Dupond-Moretti, my 'Number One' lawyer and through him, to Cherifa Benmouffok, my 'Number Two' lawyer. I thank Eric for all his hard work and dedication over the years and for taking my calls day or night, whether he wanted to or not. My thanks too go to Cherifa for her all patience and hard work on the case.

My thanks to Pearl and Michel who gave their apartment to us in Reims for the court case in 2003. I will never forget their generosity.

I thank Lara Marlowe for her support and for turning up at court with us, and also for being a wonderful and honest journalist.

I thank Reverend David Fraser for the use of his house in Laytown during the writing of this book.

I thank my wonderful sister, Noeleen Slattery, who has been there for me every step of the way, for her strength and guidance over the past nineteen years. She has been a formidable ally and a sincere friend.

I thank and remember her daughter, Caroline, for all the work she did to help us with translations and all the hospitality she gave us in her home in Chantilly.

I thank Bill for all his love and support over the years.

To Judy, Tootsie, James and William, I thank you, simply, for being wonderful children.

CONTENTS

CHAPTER 1

The Nightmare Begins

15 August 1987.

One phone call and my life was turned upside down forever.

It was about nine o'clock on that Saturday night when the phone rang. It was my daughter, Eroline, who we called Tootsie.

'Mum, don't worry too much, because I think they are wrong.'

'What are you trying to tell me?' I asked.

'I think Trevor is dead.'

Trevor was my nineteen-year-old son, a fun, handsome lad with dark good looks, a cheeky grin and a dimple in his chin. He had gone to England for the summer, his first experience of living away from home. He got work in a bar in St Albans, just north of London, where he'd become friends with another nineteen-year-old, a French lad named Christian Jaillet. Christian came from Poligny in the south east of France and had decided to return home. On a whim, Trevor decided to go to France with him. That was a week ago.

Tootsie was crying down the phone, so a friend of hers took the phone from her and spoke to me. She explained that the police had called the office where Tootsie worked, looking for her boss, a man named Kevin Sweeney. They wanted to know if Mr Sweeney or any of his family had gone to France recently.

When she asked what was wrong, the policeman, PC Barden, told her that the French police had found a dead man and that the business card of Kevin Sweeney was near the body. Tootsie had given Trevor her work number, written on the back of her boss's business card, in case he needed to contact her while he was away. She knew immediately that they were talking about Trevor.

On the other end of the phone, Tootsie tearfully took up the story of how, terrified of what she might hear, she nevertheless asked for a description of the body. PC Barden told her it was too decomposed to identify, and anyway, he said, 'it's the body of an old man'. Tootsie wasn't convinced by this explanation and went to the police station to find out more. She gave the police a photo of Trevor but they couldn't give her any further details.

Even before the visit from the police, Tootsie had been a bit concerned about Trevor. After only a few days in France, he had called her to say he was coming home because he couldn't find any work. She had expected to hear from him again on her birthday, which had just passed, but his customary 'happy birthday' call didn't come. Trevor never forgot her birthday.

My Trevor. Dead? I couldn't believe it. I put the phone down and I couldn't believe it, didn't believe it.

It just couldn't be true. My first thought was, how could I contact him to make sure he was OK? These days when I want to check where any of the family are, I can just call their mobile phones, but in 1987, it wasn't that easy. Trevor hadn't left a number for the house he was going to in France. He probably didn't even know himself where he was going. He had been to France once before but that was with a school trip to Paris when he was in primary school.

Two weeks ago, he had phoned me to say, 'I'm off to France with a mate for a few weeks, going to look for work.' I was a little surprised that he should want to go off just like that but ultimately I hadn't been overly worried and said, 'OK, sweetheart, you enjoy yourself and look after yourself too.'

Now I kept thinking back to the days before Trevor had left our home in Naas, County Kildare, to go to England. For the journey, he'd borrowed his friend's rucksack, tent and camping gear, and bought a little black beanie hat to look the part of a hitchhiker. On the day he bought the gear, he arrived into the sitting room, triumphant. 'Mum, take a few photographs of me, will you?' He often complained that there weren't enough pictures of him in the family albums and today he had new clothes and a new look to show off. He was a cheeky monkey, but young, healthy and handsome and I couldn't help looking at him and feeling proud. He posed casually in his new shirt and jeans, smiling coyly into the camera. 'You're gonna be some heartbreaker,' I laughed as I clicked. Then he donned his outdoor gear, putting the rucksack on his back, his beanie hat on his head and his brand new Walkman strung around his neck. I took the photograph in our living room, joking, 'You'll never get a lift looking like that.'

And, like any young lad, while he had bought what he considered the essentials – outdoor gear and the Walkman – it was me who stocked up on new socks, underwear and towels.

On the day of his departure, Trevor was up early, anxious to be going. I gave him breakfast along with my youngest son, William, who was only five-and-a half at the time. Trevor adored William and would probably miss him more than anyone while he was away. Bill, my partner, had already said goodbye before he went off to work. I watched as Trevor organised his rucksack and strung the earphones of his new Walkman around his neck. Looking at him, I was reminded of his first day at school. 'Stop looking at me like I'm five,' he said, catching me out. 'I'm a man now, Mum, and a man's gotta do what a man's gotta do, and all that.' We both laughed.

And now someone was trying to tell me that my beautiful young man, so full of life and expectation, was dead. It just couldn't be true. I had to do something, had to find out for myself. I called the police station in St Albans. The policeman I spoke to told me not to worry, it was not my son, he said, the person they had found was old. As much as I really wanted to believe him, somehow I didn't. I asked for the phone number of the station in France and the area where the body had been found, but, amazingly, he didn't know its name. Now what would I do?

I was frightened and at the same time angry that Trevor had gone away at all, let alone to a foreign country. I also knew that if he were dead, it was my fault. I shouldn't have let him go. Bill got the brunt of my worry and rage: 'If Trevor would just call us and tell us where he is, all this would be sorted in a heartbeat,' I railed. 'He doesn't even know we're all worrying about him. It's Saturday night, he's not going to be ringing home of his own free will on a Saturday night anyway, is he?'

Bill was more practical. 'Who else can we call?' he said.

We had run out of people to call who might know where Trevor might be. We had to find another way to contact him. I drove to Naas Garda Station and sat outside in my car, petrified. Afraid to go in and yet afraid not to. What would I find out? Was Trevor dead? How? Had he been in a car crash, had he been taken ill, an accident, a hit and run, what? It didn't seem believable, and yet I feel now that I knew it was true.

I had been happy enough about Trevor going to England because his older brother and sister were there already. James, my eldest, was spending the summer running his own rickshaw in London's Chinatown. Tootsie had two jobs in St Albans, one in an office and a part-time job in a bar. It was she who got Trevor fulltime work in the bar for the summer. He had loads of experience, having worked in bars locally around Naas since he was fifteen, but still, he was excited about the prospect of being independent for a while, being a real grown up with a bit more freedom than I would tolerate at home. In St Albans, Trevor had rented himself a room in a house and bought a bicycle to get around. He took to his new job and new-found freedom with gusto. He only came home once during the summer, with his dirty washing in tow. He stayed a few days, ate everything I gave him, got his washing done, played with William, saw a few friends, then was off again. 'Mind yourself,' I said as he left, 'see you soon.'

At the time Trevor had just finished school and was thinking about what career he would pursue. He had talked about joining the British Army but I wasn't so keen because of the Troubles in Northern Ireland and I felt that he, as a Southern Irish boy in the British Army, would be a target; that he wouldn't be safe. I couldn't bear the thought of anything happening to him. We'd had a few rows about it, but like any mother, I felt I could bring him round to my way of thinking if I just allowed him go off for the summer, let off a bit of steam. Then, when he came home after the holidays, I would sit down with him and together we'd work out just what he was going to do for the rest of his life. He was young. He had his whole life ahead of him.

All summer I had been looking forward to when Trevor would be home for good. I didn't tell him at the time, but I really missed him out of the house. I missed his banter, his fun, his cheekiness. I made a mental note to myself to make sure and spoil him a little bit extra when he came home. He was due home at the end of August and it couldn't come soon enough for me.

Eventually I got out of my car, went to the desk and spoke to the young Garda on duty. I explained that I thought my son might be dead in France and that the police in St Albans knew something about it. I asked if he would call St Albans and find out. The Garda was apologetic and could see that I was worried, but he told me he couldn't do anything and that it was 'a matter for Foreign Affairs'. I left the station and returned to my car, where I waited until it was much later, until I could see that the shift was changing and went back in again. But the same young fellow was at Reception. I asked him, please, would he call St Albans police station for me and find out what they knew. He repeated what he had said earlier, that it was a matter for Foreign Affairs.

I wasn't giving up that easily. I made more phone calls that night to St Albans. I spoke to a Sergeant Meehan who told me again that they had found a dead man and that the business card of Kevin Sweeney was near the body. I stayed by the phone in the kitchen, just in case someone rang with news.

Next morning I phoned the Department of Foreign Affairs. I was transferred to a Mr Wasser. I told him what I knew about the body being found in France and how it was suspected that it might be Trevor. He gave me the number of the Irish Embassy in Paris. I spoke to Philomena Murray there, telling her the same story. She said she would do everything she could to find out where the dead person was. After several hours, Philomena rang back to say that it was impossible for her to find out unless I knew the name of the area; I had to have a location. But I couldn't find a location.

I called the police in St Albans again to ask for the number of the police station in France. The sergeant there wouldn't give me the number, 'It's not your son,' he said, 'you're over-reacting.' I asked him again why he wouldn't give me the number. Back and forth, the conversation continued, with me asking the same question and he evading it. Eventually, he relented. 'We have difficulty with the language,' he revealed. 'There's no one here who can understand French. We don't have the spelling of the location or anything so we can't tell you where it is; we don't know it ourselves.'

I didn't know what to do then, hadn't a clue what to do next.

It was now day three. I was sleeping by the phone in the kitchen in case I missed a call. Our normal family life was put on hold for the next week as I tried to find out what I could. James and the girls were in constant contact; our conversations were always the same:

'Any news?'

'No. You?'

'No. Will call you when I hear.'

'Love you, Mum.'

'It'll be fine, sweetheart. I bet he's off on an adventure some-where.'

'Sure he is, get some sleep.'

'Love you.'

'Love you.'

I sent William to stay with a friend, and Bill was trying to keep us together, mind and body.

I phoned Paris and talked to Philomena Murray again; she could not help. She told me that she had contacted numerous police stations in France and no Irishman's body had been found. Interpol had been called but had nothing to report. She advised me to phone St Albans again to try to get the address, as that was the only way she could help me. I told her the police there couldn't speak the language, they had not understood what was being said to them and therefore had taken no notes.

I made no progress that day.

On Wednesday some policemen from Naas garda station called to my house and asked me to describe Trevor. I told them: dark, short hair, slim, very fit, handsome, a dimple in his chin, blue eyes, wearing jeans and runners or red boots.

The next day Detective Frank McLaughlin from Naas garda station called to the house. He was a trim-looking man in his early fifties with sad eyes. I knew it was bad news. He had the address and telephone number we'd been searching for. The police station was in a town called Saint-Quentin, about an hour and a half's drive northeast of Paris. More importantly, he had news on the body that had been found. It wasn't an old man as the sergeant in St Albans had insisted. His voice calm and measured, the detective told me, 'We can't confirm for sure, but it could be Trevor.'

I had to get to France. I phoned the police in Saint-Quentin to tell them I was coming and, although I should have been expecting it, was actually shocked when they answered in French. As soon as I started speaking, they knew who I was.

I had nothing like the amount of money I would need for the journey. I was in a panic. What was I going to do? I needed to get to France as soon as possible. Who could I turn to for money? Who did I know with ready access to cash? Suddenly I thought of Mick Fitzpatrick, the local milkman. I knew Mick socially from around the town and his son was in the same class as my youngest boy, William. Mick was my only hope. It was Thursday afternoon and Mick would be collecting the week's milk money from around the housing estates in Naas. I got into my car and went looking for him. I found him on his milk round nearby. I asked him for six hundred pounds, telling him about the news from France and that I thought it might be Trevor. He didn't have that amount collected yet but told me to meet him later at a housing estate called Lacken View in Naas when he would have more money. I caught up with him two hours later. He handed over the money and wished me luck. It was an extraordinary thing for him to loan me, an acquaintance, that amount of money, but he never even hesitated.

I phoned Aer Lingus and booked the only seat available – a first class return ticket that cost £500. I would have to change at Heathrow airport in London as there were no direct flights available. The flight was departing in two days time, Saturday, 22 August. Next I had to get a passport.

I didn't have a passport, had never been abroad and had never needed it. I'd been to England several times to visit my sister, Daphne, but that was as far as I ever went. Who to ask? I hadn't been in touch with my oldest sister, Noeleen, for years – not for any particular reason – we didn't live near each other and we had each just been getting on with our own lives and families. But I did remember that her ex husband, Paddy Slattery, was a policeman. Would he know how to get a passport, especially at such short notice?

I hardly knew him at all, but I got his number somehow and asked him to help. He said he would do what he could for me. He arranged to meet me in Dublin on Saturday, the day of the flight. I organised for William to stay with my good friend, Jane, kissed him goodbye on Saturday morning and headed for Dublin. I'd brought a photo with me, as instructed, and we went to the Passport Office. Even though the office was officially closed, as it was a Saturday, Paddy had arranged for someone to be there specially to process my passport. I couldn't have been more grateful to Paddy for his help. The whole thing took only a very short time and, armed with my brand-new passport, I went to meet Bill, who was driving me to the airpport.

Bill got me checked in at the flight desk and we said our good-byes. I gave him a list of things to do while I was gone, including people to call and family to contact and update with what was happening. 'Have you got everything?' I asked him. 'Yes,' he replied, then hugged me and whispered that I would be fine; I was strong, and that maybe, hopefully, it wasn't Trevor at all. 'I'll call you,' I said. 'As soon as I know.'

I sat down in my seat on the plane. It was then I started to shake. I had no idea where I was going, no idea how long I would be away. Worse still, I had no idea how I was going to deal with whatever was ahead of me in France. A week ago my daughter had called me with the unbelievable news that my son might be dead. Just like that. Time worked into shifts, sleeping by the telephone, awaking then to make calls, waiting, waiting, waiting for any news from any quarter. Now here I was, on my way to identify what was probably the body of my son who was lying in a morgue somewhere outside Paris. Trevor. Dead. The stewards came round with free drinks. Two men seated next to me said, 'Go on, have a drink, you look like you need one.' I had a brandy but didn't return their chat. I couldn't.

One of the men asked if I was going on my holidays. 'No,' I said, but I didn't elaborate.

I arrived in Charles De Gaulle airport on Saturday evening. I didn't have much luggage. I had told James the number of my flight and he was arranging to come by ferry from England. In the meantime, Noeleen's ex-husband had got in touch with her. She was in Deauville, in northern France, with her daughter, Caroline, the only professional lady jockey in France at the time, who was riding in the Deauville race meeting. Noeleen was on holiday, meeting the racing circuit's rich and famous, including Omar Sharif, when she got the call about Trevor. She and Caroline dropped everything and were on their way to Paris by car. I waited at the taxi rank for them. It got very dark and still I was walking up and down, up and down the taxi rank. Every new taxi-man who joined the rank approached me, asking, 'Taxi?, Taxi?' No, I told them, no, no. They must have thought I was mad. Three, four, then five hours went by. Eventually Noeleen arrived with Caroline. We had to pick up James, which meant driving north to one of the ports before doubling back south again for Saint-Quentin, 132km northeast of Paris, in the Picardie region of France.

I might as well have been going to the moon; I had not the slightest idea how far we had to travel. We drove all night. We stopped and had something to eat. It was a strange journey in more ways than one. I hadn't seen or spoken to my sister for years. I had seen Caroline only once or twice since she was a child, so it was almost as though James and I were travelling with two strangers. But there was no awkwardness; the circumstances and the close quarters of Caroline's little car bonded us, and James and I told them everything we knew. We arrived in Saint-Quentin at around two o'clock the next morning and found the gates to the police station locked. In the moonlight the station looked enormous and foreboding behind high double railings. We had to identify ourselves by an intercom. The gates swung open and we went in.

Inside, the building was old, with long low-lit corridors. The police were expecting us. The two senior officers, a captain and a constable, had no English at all, so they had arranged for a young conscript with some English to ask the questions. All were dressed impeccably in the dark navy uniform of the gendarmerie and, despite the late hour, the meeting was stiff and formal. Through the young conscript, they asked what Trevor looked like – his height, his weight. Then they asked what he might have been wearing. Did he drink? Did he smoke? Why did he go to France? They questioned us for a number of hours and then asked what we thought were stupid questions, really. Why had he left home? Why had he been staying with a young man? Did he have many male friends? I felt they were trying to imply that Trevor was homosexual and couldn't understand why they should do this or why it might be important to them.

Captain Alain Skoczylas, a tall, imposing man, was in charge of the investigation. He brought out some items that had been found on the body: runners, socks, a watch, still working, and asked if I could identify them. They were all Trevor's. You would think that this would have been proof enough for me that Trevor was dead, but it all felt unreal. Even though I was taking in everything that was happening, a part of me still didn't believe Trevor was dead, didn't want to believe it. Sure, I was answering questions about him, I was even identifying some of his possessions, but deep down I wasn't fully making the connection.

Then the captain showed us six or seven photographs of a body that had been buried in undergrowth. Each photograph depicted the uncovering of the body, limb by limb. The first photograph showed a hand. It was Trevor's hand. I also recognised his watch, a clockwork Citizen watch I had given him and which the policeman had just shown to me a while before. The next photographs revealed more of the body. It was Trevor. I recognised him immediately. How could I not? He was my son. I knew his hair, knew his teeth. I was numb. This could not be happening to our family. My son. I needed to see my son. I wouldn't believe he was really dead until I had seen the body.

While the young conscript tried his best, it was actually Caroline, Noeleen's daughter, who was providing the translations between Captain Skoczylas and me. I told her to ask if I could see the body. He hesitated, and then he said that it was not possible: the body had been buried the day before, on the order of the investigating magistrate. We all gasped. I felt as though someone had hit me. How could they have done this? They knew I was coming to identify the body, so why had they buried him? I just couldn't understand it. Caroline threw her hands up in the air and in French said, 'You buried him?' The police looked at each other. Their only explanation was that it was too hot and the Saint-Quentin hospital mortuary was not equipped to keep bodies for more than four days!

James, my son, lost it. He kicked the wall in rage. We had been on tenterhooks for days; no sleep, staying by the phone in case anyone rang with news, calling everyone we could think of who might help, not knowing if it was Trevor's body that had been found, hoping it wasn't him and that he was alive and well somewhere, anywhere. Then, finding out that it probably was Trevor's body they had found, the journey to France, travelling all night, knowing we were going to identify my son's body. After all the uncertainty of the last week, we at least expected to see him one last time.

My head was swimming, but all I could do now was try and mind James, look after him and try to get him calmed down. I took him in my arms. But the police had yet another shock in store for us.

Captain Skoczylas said that Trevor had been murdered. Although it may seem naive now, somehow it had never crossed my mind that my son had been murdered. Who would want to kill Trevor? I thought it was an accident of some kind. The police captain told us that Trevor's body had been discovered on 8 August and that he had been strangled, possibly by a strap or cord. An autopsy had been ordered on 11 August to determine precisely when and how the death had occurred. In Captain Skoczylas's opinion, Trevor's killing had probably been motivated by robbery; there were people robbing hitchhikers all the time. He told us that Trevor probably died very quickly, though I thought he was trying to make the news somehow easier for me. I couldn't take it all in. Trevor was dead, and now I was finding out that he was murdered.

Years later, I found out that the region where Trevor had been found was known as 'The Triangle of Death' because of the number of young men who had disappeared there. It was suspected that there was a serial killer on the loose in the area. Was Captain Skoczylas aware of this? It would seem incredible if he was not, yet he certainly never made any mention of it to us that night. What he did promise was that he would do everything to catch my son's killer.

The captain had booked a hotel for us and the police escorted us there. We followed behind their car. The three of us women shared a room and James had his own room. We didn't sleep. There was too much to take in. The shock was enormous and all we could do was talk all night long. How could this happen? What were we going to do? How were we going to do it? Who did we need to help us? One thing was certain, I was determined to bring Trevor home with me, no matter what. I couldn't bear the thought of him alone in some grave somewhere. Noeleen's calm quiet voice broke through the din: 'We have to keep our heads about us.' She would have no idea just how right she was; none of us knew just what it was we were facing into.

The next morning at breakfast we were aware of the hotel owners watching us and talking about us. It was a small hotel and they obviously knew who we were since the police had booked the rooms for us. Eventually they treaded softly towards us with the local newspaper and pointed to a small article. It was only a few lines but mentioned a body being found. We thanked them for it, but we didn't really know how to react. Noeleen said, 'let's just keep our heads down from now on.'

We went back to the police station. If I couldn't see the body, then I was determined at least to see where Trevor had been found. I asked to see the site. The police drove us to a largely flat rural locality called Les Sablonnières, near Alaincourt. It was 10km from Saint-Quentin, off the main A26 north/south autoroute. Saint-Quentin's industrial suburbs trailed behind us as we journeyed out past warehouses and factories into the countryside. We continued miles off the main road, down a long and twisted lane, with pot-holes full of muck on the edge of cornfields. Featureless and indis-tinguishable, I thought to myself, there's not even a landmark to find the place again. It was so far away from anywhere and I remember thinking how could anyone find their way here? We were well off the tourist trail, halfway between Paris and the Bel-gian border, a nowhere's land. I couldn't imagine Trevor actually making any effort at all to come here. Someone must have brought him here. And whoever it was, they knew how to get here, knew the area, and, I decided, did not expect him to be found, ever.

The police introduced us to Michel Lente, a local farmer and the person who had found Trevor. Tall and unprepossessing, Michel Lente could only shake his head in sorrow. I took his hand in mine, 'Thank you,' I said, 'thank you so much.' I was so grateful to him, even if I couldn't communicate it in his own language to him. I really believe it was a miracle that Trevor was found at all. Had it been even a month or two later and coming into winter, he would never have been found. At least Trevor's body had been recovered.

I then asked to see where Trevor was buried and the police told us it was in the local cemetery, La Tombelle. We drove back towards Saint-Quentin and into a huge municipal cemetery with long grass verges edged with pretty flowerbeds. However, we didn't stop here but continued on towards the back of the grave-yard where we came to a halt. The police got out of their car and walked ahead of us. No longer green-grassed and flower-edged, this part of the cemetery was completely bare, save for a few strag-gly poplar trees marking its boundary. Known as the pauper's space, its unmarked mounds of earth were separated only by make-shift muck paths. The police pointed to one of these mounds as being the one we wanted. On the newly dug grave, such as it was, there was no cross or any identification at all. It was just a hole in the ground, filled in. It was desolate. I thought of Trevor, posing in his brand new clothes at the beginning of the summer, only a few short months ago, and how gleaming and new he looked. The summer lay like a great big adventure before him. Now, standing in mud, looking at a muck-filled grave at the paupers' backend of a cemetery, I determined that this was not where my beautiful gleaming son would spend a moment longer.

We left and went back to the station. The police told us to go home and they would get in touch with me. But I said no, we would wait and take Trevor home. 'We are not going without my son,' I said firmly. James struggled to keep calm and I moved close, just in front of him, between him and the police. We asked to see the judge who advised them to bury Trevor, but she was too busy to see us. We walked up and down outside her office, waited for a few hours and then asked again to see her. Still, she was too busy.

We didn't know what we were going to do now. I thought that, surely, as the body had now been identified as Trevor's, an Irish citizen, Foreign Affairs would be able to help us. So I found a phone box on the street and rang them a number of times during that day and then again the next day, but to no avail. Caroline had to go back to Deauville and James had to return to England. Noeleen and I stayed on and wandered the streets of Saint-Quentin, a town three times the size of Naas, on the banks of the river Somme. We talked and talked as we walked, trying to make sense of it all. One question haunted me. Why would anyone want to harm my child, my Trevor?

Only one week before, I had been working in Atlantic Home-care, selling lawn-mowers, doing ordinary everyday things. I was going to paint the house. My family were working away happily in their various jobs here and there. Everything in my world seemed fine and normal. But I was wrong, because, unbelievably, what was actually happening was that my beautiful young son was being brutally strangled to death and his body was being buried in the back of beyond in a foreign country. And now, just a week later, I was having to deal with bureaucracy, policemen, the law, in a language I didn't have a word of, in a town I didn't know, in a country I'd never been to.

It was now four days since we had come to France and I was still determined not to leave without Trevor, but Captain Skoczylas said we must go home. He told us that it would take weeks to get the order we needed to have Trevor's body exhumed and flown home. And we would need a lawyer to organise the exhumation order. He was unequivocal. What else could we do? We had to go home. It was now 26 August, the end of the summer. This was the time I had been expecting my son to come home to me from his travels. Instead I was abandoning him abroad, leaving him behind in that desolate gravesite. I would never forgive myself.

The day after we came home without Trevor, I walked down the street on the lefthand side of Naas and went into every single law office and asked to see the solicitor. I had no appointment, so I was asked what it was in connection with. What problem did I need to discuss? I wouldn't tell them. I asked if the owner, solicitor or staff knew anything about French law. The answer in every case was no. So I crossed over the road and called to every solicitor's office on the righthand side of the street. The result was the same: no one knew French law or spoke French. I went home. It was now five or maybe six in the evening. I rang the Law Society in Blackhall Place and left my number. At around ten o'clock that night, someone from the Law Society phoned back and gave me the number of Garrett Sheehan in Francis Street, Dublin. The next day I spoke to Garrett Sheehan on the phone and told him I had a problem. Noeleen and myself went to his office that evening for a six o'clock appointment. We explained about the murder of Trevor, what had happened when we went to France, and asked what needed to be done now. He told us of a colleague of his, Barrister Patrick McEntee, who was in Paris, working on another Irishman's case, and that he would get in touch with him that evening. He also knew a French lawyer in Paris who he was sure would help; his name was Antoine Comte. Next morning, Garrett Sheehan phoned and asked us back to his office. He had been in touch with Paddy McEntee, who was going to help us get Trevor exhumed as soon as possible, with the assistance of Antoine Comte.

Already the bills were mounting and I was worried about how I was going to pay. I phoned Foreign Affairs to find out if there was any way they could help with money to bring Trevor home. I felt that perhaps the Government would have something in place to help people like me in this situation, where a loved one is murdered abroad and their body has to be flown home. But they couldn't help, it wasn't in their power to help in this way. 'Do you know how big France is and how many murders there are in the country, and if we were to pay to bring back every dead body from abroad, how costly that would be?' they said. They weren't aggressive about it, they were just amused that I should even ask, because the State didn't have any mechanism to help people in this situation. Even today there is nothing in place if this happens to a family. I know that there are often cases where a foreigner who is murdered in Ireland will be flown home and their family's expenses paid for by the Irish Government. But these situations are subject to the Criminal Injuries Compensation Tribunal and an Irish citizen who sustains criminally inflicted injuries abroad cannot claim to this tribunal. I was on my own.

It would be a year later, in 1988, when I learnt that under French law there is a system whereby a victim (or their family) of an offence that resulted in severe physical damage or death can claim compensation. However, in the case of claimants who are not French citizens, it is necessary to prove that their country of origin has signed a reciprocal agreement with France. Ireland had not signed any such agreement, but, through my Irish lawyer, Garret Sheehan, and my French lawyer, Antoine Comte, I applied for compensaion anyway, and hoped that it would be successful. The compensation was indeed paid out, although not until 1995, eight years after I brought Trevor home.

When we came back from France that first time, all we could do was wait for the lawyers to get the exhumation order organised. Days crawled into weeks. Irish newspapers picked up on the story of the young Irishman murdered abroad. I didn't talk to any of them, but it didn't stop them reporting all sorts of stories, many of which were untrue. Some of the papers described Trevor as being found half naked. Although I knew he hadn't been half naked, I went mad thinking about the indignity of it, of people reading about it, and believing it, people we knew and Trevor knew: class-mates, girlfriends, punters in the bars where he worked. I had terrible dreams where Trevor was begging me to cover him up. Over and over again, he kept saying to me, 'Mum, cover me up, cover me up.'

A few times when reporters came to the door, I pretended I was the housekeeper. I didn't want anyone to know. I didn't want to talk about what had happened Trevor; I felt I barely knew all the details myself. But most of all, I had to protect my family, to protect Trevor's dignity, and I had to look after the others, mind them, make sure no harm came to them. James and Tootsie came back from England; Judy, my eldest daughter, came back from New Zealand and we all looked after little William. The kids were traumatised. Noeleen travelled every day from her home, 13km away in Rathcoole. She was the strong one, the person to lean on. She was my crutch and through all these years she has always been there for me. My other brothers and sisters were there too and they all pitched in to help with money and time as best they could. With both the kids and my siblings around, the house was consolably full and distracting.

Weeks of waiting came to an end when finally, on 29 September, authorisation was given for Trevor's body to be exhumed for transport back to Ireland. Noeleen and myself went back to Saint-Quentin to take Trevor home. I had to sign the exhumation order to bring him home and which was also signed by J F Pioche, Commissioner de Police, Saint-Quentin. I had wanted to have Trevor's body cremated in France and bring the ashes home for burial in Ireland. However, the police had insisted that I sign papers that if Trevor's body were required again, he would be exhumed in

Ireland, which meant he couldn't be cremated.

Before we left France in August, we had gone to an undertakers to arrange Trevor's funeral. While we hadn't been able to specify a date, we had put in an order for a coffin and the undertaker said it would cost about £1,000, possibly more, but I'm sure it wasn't less. I remember that he would only accept a bank draft or cash. When we got back to Ireland, Noeleen went guarantor for me at the Bank of Ireland for any money I would need. I also used the loan to pay back the milkman, Mick Fitzpatrick.

When we arrived in Saint-Quentin, we went to the Hotel de Guise, the same hotel where we had stayed on our first visit. It was on a street not far from the old town square. The police had placed a young policeman, Hervé, at our disposal as a translator; he hadn't much English but just enough to help us.

We went immediately to the undertaker and told him Trevor's funeral arrangements. I had the bank draft ready to pay him but then the undertaker told us he had no coffin. We needed a lead coffin within a coffin to comply with regulations regarding taking a body on a plane. While the undertaker said that he didn't have one available, we got the distinct impression that if we offered more money a suitable coffin could be found. Noeleen suggested we find another undertaker. Hervé conveyed to us that the undertaker didn't want to lose the custom, and, sure enough, by the next day he had located the required coffin to take Trevor home. However, the coffin had to be sent down from Paris, and so would take a day or two. More delay.

That night, Hervé found us a restaurant and joined us for dinner. He even told us a few jokes in his broken English to lighten the mood. It was one of the kindest acts anyone had shown us since the whole nightmare had begun. That night we laughed in spite of how we felt. The following day was to be the most horrendous yet.

We awoke to pouring rain. Noeleen was driving Caroline's car, which she had loaned to her mum. It was almost midday when we arrived at La Tombelle cemetery. It was the day of the exhumation and, for legal reasons, one of us had to witness it. Although we had not much idea what exactly was involved, other than that the coffin would be removed from the grave, we had a long discussion about who would act as witness. I said I would. Noeleen said she would. Eventually we agreed that Noeleen would do it and that I would stand nearby but not look.

We both got out of the car and stood by the graveside. I looked the other way. But, as the JCB digger wheeled into position and began removing the earth from the grave, I couldn't let Noeleen do it alone. I said, 'I'll do it with you; I want to look'. 'You're sure?' she asked me. 'I'm sure,' I replied.

There were four or five men, including the graveyard caretaker – a young man in his early twenties – along with the JCB and a small black van. No one spoke to us. Eventually the soil was removed and the coffin was brought up into view. It was not at all what we expected. The coffin, such as it was, was made of the poorest wood: a crude square box of floorboards, tongue and groove wood, and it was even broken in places. A large plastic bag, like a refuse sack, gaped through the broken wood. The smell was overpowering. I was appalled.

Noeleen and I both reeled back, disgusted and humiliated. This was my son, in a plastic bag, in a makeshift box. When the coffin was raised, I noticed bluebottles buzzing around it in their droves even though it was raining. The men looked at them but never spoke. They manoeuvred the coffin into the black van and drove away, leaving Noeleen and I alone in the empty cemetery.

Silently, sorrowfully, we drove the car back to Caroline's house in Chantilly where she took us to the airport and we said our good-byes. Trevor's body was transferred to the coffins I had ordered but we were not on the same flight because of passenger and weight restrictions. We went on one airplane and his body went via another carrier. When we landed in Dublin we went to the airport mortuary where some friends and family had already gathered. We said a few prayers, glad to be home and away from that dreadful grave. Try as I might, I could not get the picture of the plastic bag and broken makeshift coffin out of my head. Angry and embarrassed, I couldn't even bring myself to say anything to anyone about it either, not even to Noeleen.

The funeral cortege arrived in Naas at 10pm on 1 October 1987. The burial was after 10am Mass the next day. We had placed notices in the local papers and the church was packed with family and friends. The media had also reported the funeral details and some reporters turned up at the church. We walked from the Church of Our Lady and St David in Naas to St Corbin's grave-yard. I was sure I saw dirty big bluebottles buzzing over the coffin in the church and I was convinced I could hear them buzzing around the grave as it was finally filled in and Trevor's body was laid to rest. 'Those flies have followed us all the way from France,' I said to Noeleen. 'Shh ... ' she said gently as she took my arm to lead me from the grave.

Jimmy – Trevor's dad and my estranged husband – had come for the funeral from his home in England. Jimmy arrived late, and when the funeral was over I had to give him his fare back to

England as he had only bought a one-way ticket. It was typical of him, but at least he had made the effort.

The funeral took place a full six weeks after we had first gone to Saint-Quentin to bring Trevor home. Finally, I had been able to cover him up.

CHAPTER 2

A Wonderful Son, Brother, Nephew

The first time I saw Trevor was on 6 November 1967. I was twenty-two years old and he had just been born. When the nurses handed him to me and I saw the great big dimple in his chin, I thought he looked dreadful! 'Oh, my God,' I said, 'he's awful looking!' The nurses whisked him away in a shot because they thought maybe I didn't like him. Of course I liked him, I loved him; I loved all my babies. I just needed to get over the shock of this huge dimple. Soon enough I declared to the world that he was gorgeous and I called him after an actor I liked at the time: Trevor Howard, star of the film *Brief Encounter*. Trevor was my fourth child. My kids were all steps of stairs in age, less than a year between each of them. It made them close. Then there was a fifteen-year gap between Trevor and the youngest, William, with my partner, Bill.

I had been brought up in a large family in Dublin and things were scare. My mother would fry a rasher for my father's tea and there would be grease on the pan into which we were allowed dip our bread, but we had to be sure to leave the bacon for Daddy. We used to say, 'Dip in the drip and leave the rasher for Daddy'. And even that was a big treat! There were ten of us, five boys and five girls. I left school at twelve or thirteen and went to work pulling cabbages. Noeleen, being the eldest, probably got the best education; she got to stay in school until she was sixteen but the rest of us had to go out to work. We had no choice. Our mother got TB, and myself, my twin sister Charlotte and younger sister June were put into an orphanage because my father couldn't cope with us. I was eleven years old at the time. We were there for two years until Mammy got better and came back for us. She always dressed the three of us in the same outfits and somebody once asked if we were triplets. 'Oh yes,' said my mother, 'and only fifteen months between them!'

Mammy was warm and funny and solidly loyal. She was to be a great help to me in the years when I was on my own with four kids to bring up single-handedly. She'd send something to the kids and me whenever she could. When she died, in 1975, it was a great loss to me and the rest of my siblings.

Daddy, on the other hand, was a strict disciplinarian. He was also a man of his time and certainly wouldn't have approved of separation in marriage and suchlike. However he was dogged and focused in whatever he undertook and never wavered in any way. He believed in doing the right thing and was very supportive of my battle to bring my son's killer to court, right up until he died six years ago. He was living in Swords and wasn't in good health for the last twenty-five years of his life, but whenever he had a major health setback he would come to me to convalesce and it was then he would catch up on Trevor's case and what we were doing to progress it.

I was nearly nineteen when I got married in 1963. In those days it didn't seem young; you married to have sex! I married Jimmy O'Keeffe. He was in the Air Corps in Baldonnel. He was very attractive. All the girls fancied him but it was me who married him. He was as tall and dark as I was slim and blonde and we did look great as a couple. Unfortunately, marriage didn't agree with Jimmy and we soon separated, but not before I had four little babies, all one after the other, barely thirteen months between births. The kids being so close in age helped them become good friends grow-ing up. They always looked out for each other and that made me so proud of them. Jimmy left when Trevor was three and from then on I was on my own. It was the early Seventies and I didn't know any other separated people. I was determined the kids wouldn't suffer and I would be the best Mummy and Daddy I could be for them. I worked as hard as I could and every little thing I did with them I presented as a big adventure.

We didn't have a lot of money but we had loads of fun.

I had two girls, Judy and Eroline Jnr. who we called Tootsie, then a boy, James, and now Trevor. I was delighted to have another boy. I always thought I'd have lots of boys, though I was never dis-appointed with Judy and Tootsie. Trevor was so much smaller than the other three and even small for his age. He was a slight little fellow with lovely, dark wavy hair and quick blue eyes that always made him look like he was up to mischief. And generally he was.

He was cheeky but charming with it. No matter what chore you asked him to do, he would have an answer for you as to why it shouldn't be him, quick as lightning. I would ask him to bring in a bucket of coal for the fire from the shed outside and before I'd even finished the request he'd say, 'why can't you ask James?' Then James would say, 'you never ask Trevor to do anything.' It was true, because Trevor could always get himself out of whatever needed doing, some way or another.

At that time, we lived in a neat little housing estate in Saggart, County Dublin, which was very much a country area, not at all built up like it is today. There were fields all around and I sent all my kids to the national school there before the regular school age of four. Even though I was working, I couldn't afford to pay someone to look after them. So on Judy's first day at school she was only three years and nine months and I had three others toddling about at that stage, Trevor being the baby.

I bought a great big Silver Cross pram in Pa Keogh's shop in Rathcoole and got it 'off the drip' for two shillings and sixpence a month. It was just about big enough to take all four kids at the same time and looked like a bouncing nest of baby birds, all tufted little heads and pink cheeks squawking. Judy would be balanced on the outside of the pram, Trevor nestled at the bottom, but side over so he could breathe, and the other two perched on the top of it! It was a squeeze for them and a push for me, but at least they were all contained and baby Trevor was kept warm by the rest of his siblings.

When it came time for Trevor to go to primary school, he took to it like a duck to water while I was left with an empty nest. Each morning I would bring all the children across the road outside our house, taking Trevor's little hand in mine as we crossed over to the same side of the street as the school; from there it was only a fifteen-minute walk. He went with his brother and sisters, all linking hands as they meandered along the road. In those days there was no such thing as a 'school run', everyone just walked!

For us five, the years swept by in shift-work for me and times-tables for them. I was working flexible hours in the hotel trade so that I could be around for the kids as much as possible but still have enough money coming in. I worked during school hours and nights. It was always a juggling act but I managed, just about.

The kids all liked school. They didn't get into trouble, although Trevor did mitch off school once. I knew nothing about it for a whole week. He was about six and James was a year older. The two of them stole off to the football field at the back of the school, played a top secret game of soccer and then scoffed their sandwiches in the shed at the end of the field. They weren't alone; my two little rebels were joined by about seven or eight other fugitives, all mitching class on the same day. As a tactic, such a large absentee rate was sure to be rumbled, yet the band of football renegades stayed down the field undetected until school was over. The next day, however, was a different story and there was hell to pay when they turned up to school and encountered the wrath of the headmaster. It wasn't until a week later that I found out. I immediately grounded Trevor and James. I couldn't have doled out a more severe punishment as they were forced to watch their friends as they played up and down the street from the confines of the living room. I don't think they ever mitched again.

Trevor always had loads of friends. There was a little gang of them who pitched tents in the back garden in the summertime – like boy scouts. It was a big adventure to camp out overnight. As dusk fell, a group of five or six boys would settle into the tents, zipped into their sleeping bags and telling gory ghost stories, their impish little faces lit with the flashlamps from their bicycles. From the kitchen I'd hear the rise and fall of their staged whispers as they recounted blood-curdling stories of banshees in the bushes, and ghouls in the coal shed. There would be a collective hush to listen for any scary lurkers outside. I always made sure the back door was open so that they could come back indoors if they got frightened.

In school and out of it, Trevor was the one who could cause a row, and James, who was so much bigger than him, would have to wade in to sort out the mess. 'I'll get my big brother to you,' Trevor would say and draft in James to help him. Outside in the street, they backed each other to the hilt. Inside, they fought and argued to the last. I'm sure I only ever heard the half of it. Arguments ranged from the stupid to the trivial. I used to get jumpers knitted for the children when they were little, and to save money I would get four done at the same time. This inevitably caused rows as to who owned which jumper. Even identifying them by size was difficult since they were only half-inches apart. Still, wearing someone else's sweater was a gross offence. As the years passed, Trevor would also have to wear James's cast-offs. He hated it. 'I'm not wearing his trousers,' he'd yell, 'and I'm not wearing his jumper either.'

All my kids loved sports and being fit. Judy was into girls' football, which was only starting then, her pigtails flying as she raced up and down the pitch after the ball. It was the late 1970s. James liked cross-country running, but it was Trevor who loved sports the most. He played football, soccer and Gaelic football as well as being involved in cycling and running. He ran cross-country and often won races despite being such a skinny boy. He also started karate when he was eleven or twelve, and he was very good at it. Every Saturday for years and in all weathers I'd race back from work to make it to the evening soccer match. I would see Trevor, all shining eyes and shirt flapping, and he'd be looking out for me on the sideline. I didn't like football that much but I wouldn't miss it if I could help it.

Our house became a home for all manner of lost and foundling animals as the kids showed off their caring natures. Perched on the edge of a housing estate with a field right beside it, we were ideally placed as a sanctuary. There were animals everywhere. We had hamsters and guinea pigs inside, pigeons and hens outside. We also had a goat that we got when she was a kid. We called her Betsy and she was ditsy. She would escape onto the road, chasing cars through the estate, just like a dog. Trevor loved Betsy and was great at minding her, although she was well able to feed herself, helping herself to the best of our neighbours' gardens! Eventually though, Betsy got too big and we had to give her away. Trevor was distraught. The neighbours were delighted.

We didn't have much for luxuries, but in 1979 we had enough money to go on our first holiday. I bought a mobile home and I put it in Paddy Murphy's field in Curracloe, County Wexford for £100 a year. That was our holidays for the next few years. I had an old battered Mini that was our freedom and escape; we'd throw everything into it and then drive down to Wexford. It was great fun. We'd go on a Friday evening after school and come back on a Sunday, summer and winter. When we got there we'd go straight down to the beach and I'd teach the kids to drive on the sand. We'd inevitably end up in the sand dunes or get stuck in sinking sand. Luckily the Mini was so light – it didn't even have much of a floor – so that when it did get stuck, we'd all pitch in together and lift it back out again. I taught all my kids to drive and I loved the idea of the independence it would give them later on. When it came to Trevor's turn, we'd put a cushion under him so he could look over the steering wheel. He could actually reach the pedals by the age of ten and I was proud as punch of him.

On a good day, the Wexford beach might be packed with people, and rather than wade through the crowds, we'd take off in the car. We loved the open road. Along the way we'd stop to get out and go for a walk. We'd clamber up a mountain or cut through some fields. I'd always find something for us to do, especially something for which we didn't have to pay. To us, even the most mundane outing was a big adventure. We'd go into a field and pull a cabbage, or all spread out in a field of spuds and bring out enough for tea. Nobody ever seemed to mind us going into the fields, though they might have, had they caught us! We raced out of the fields, arms laden, hearts pumping, loaded the car and when it was cooked up, we ate our plunder with glee. Sometimes we'd go robbing orchards. I loved robbing orchards. I still would, only I'm too old! And anyway there are no orchards now, not like there used to be. Back then, we'd help each other over walls and ditches, up trees and along branches to knock the fruit to the ground. We'd fill our pockets and scarper. We were a fit and fast family, like a well-oiled machine.

Trevor loved fishing, too, so sometimes we'd go to a trout farm so he could fish. The only snag was that every fish caught had to be paid for. The fish would be so starving they would virtually hurl themselves out of the water when they saw the bait. Four of us watched as Trevor cast his line out into the heaving pond. 'Try not to catch too many,' I'd encourage him, 'or at least if you do, try not to let the warden see you reel them in.'

It was Trevor's last year in primary school and I allowed him to go on a school trip abroad. It was to be his first journey out of Ireland. He was going to France, to Paris, and it was a big deal to him, and to the rest of the family too. None of us, myself included, had ever been outside of Ireland at that stage, so there was much excitement in our house in preparation for the trip. First off I had to get him a passport and then exchange Irish pounds for francs for his spending money. Trevor loved having his own passport; you could see the thrill he got from opening it and looking at his picture. It made him feel really grown up, like a big fellow. After weeks of talking of little else, the day came for him to leave and we all went down to the school to see him off. To look at the five of us waving at the bus, you'd think he was emigrating. When he came back, after three or four days, he was full of stories about his travels. He had taken in every little detail of where they'd been and what they had seen. Boulevards and old buildings, the Champs Élysées and L'Arc de Triomphe, he remembered all the names and reeled them off to us in an exaggerated accent. He brought me a present which he'd bought with his own money – a souvenir plastic Eiffel Tower. It was the ugliest thing imaginable. And I had specifically told him not to spend his money on stupid souvenirs, that they were a waste of money. The very thing I told him not to do, he did. I still have it.

Not long afterwards, my house burned down through a freak accident. We had gone out for the day and came back and got busy with our chores. I was in the kitchen and Tootsie was lighting the gas fire, but the gas bottle had leaked onto the floor, and as she lit the pilot light, the whole thing exploded. Poor Tootsie had her hair singed off but I ushered us all out unscathed. Two cats died through smoke inhalation, but we were very lucky really. However, I lost almost all our photographs of the family: all the kids as babies, all our holiday photos, shots of Trevor as a baby, his First Communion, his first trip abroad, all gone. I didn't worry too much about the house but the loss of the photographs was immeasurable. I mourned their loss for days.

We were re-housed while our own house underwent renovation.

I told the kids it was just another big adventure for us. I got them excited about the move to a new house and new neighbourhood. However, the temporary house turned out to be an eight-berth mobile home right beside the old house. It was great fun for the first while but so much smaller than our own house and we were all living on top of each other. So it was a difficult job to keep the excitement of our big adventure going after a while!

We settled back into a more normal routine after the house had been renovated and returned to its pre-fire state. Trevor finished primary school in Saggart and went to Moylepark in Clondalkin for secondary school. By now it was 1980. Secondary school for the most part passed unremarkably except for two incidents that seriously worried me. It was the middle of winter. Trevor was thirteen. He got a throat infection that became worse; his tonsils swelled up so much that one night our family doctor had to perform a tracheotomy on him before driving him to the hospital. I thought he was going to die. Instead, after three weeks he made a full recovery and not only that, he fell in love. The day came for him to leave hospital and I was ready with the car to take him home. He started to cry, saying he didn't want to go home. I couldn't understand his behaviour until a pretty young nurse arrived to tell him he had to go home but that he could write to her! As soon as he got home he did write. I suppose she was his first love and it was so innocent.

It was also around that time that Trevor went on a football trip to Mosney. All the boys jumped into the swimming pool and were larking around. Trevor got into difficulties. One of the other mothers spotted him just in time and he was rescued. She said he could have drowned. He'd had two lucky escapes in so many months. I started to think of him as the cat with nine lives.

As he got older, Trevor got bigger, almost shot up in height and build. He loved it when he started to pass me out and was taller than me. He would ask me to take off my high-heeled shoes, then he would stand alongside me, towering over me, and, smiling down, he'd call me 'Small Fry'. He was still cheeky but also became a happy-go-lucky lad. If the roof fell in, he wouldn't make a fuss over it; he took everything in his stride. He never went through that terrible teenage angst that other kids go through. In fact, I was lucky that all the kids were very good. And if by any chance at all they weren't, they had me to answer to! Judy, the eldest, was a great housekeeper and good at minding the rest of the kids. Even though she was only fractionally older than the others, they would do as she told them or she would sort them out. She was a great second mummy!

As the years rolled on, the family became very self-sufficient, with one exception, of course. Trevor never learned to cook. He couldn't even boil an egg and had no interest in it. If he wanted something to eat at four o'clock in the day and I wasn't around, he'd make porridge. It was the easiest thing for him to cook. He would wait patiently for one of his older sisters to come home so they would make something for him. Trevor always got what Trevor wanted.

Christmas was a big occasion in our house and all Trevor ever wanted from Santa was 'Action Man' toys. I would spend ages looking for new accessories for his Action Man characters so I could surprise him with them. But by the time he received whatever new gadget or toy off Santa on Christmas morning, he would have already known what he was getting. All the kids did. They took great delight in telling me years later that they all knew what presents they were getting because they had found where I was hiding them.

I still have Trevor's favourite toys – the Action Man characters. I kept them in his room for years after he died, then, gradually, after a few years, had the courage to move them out from his room into a cupboard. Now they're down in the garage.

In 1982 William was born. Trevor was then fifteen. Trevor adored the new baby and looked on him as a little toy to play with. He loved the fact that he was no longer the youngest and now there was someone *he* could spoil rotten. When William was only a few months old, we got a frame and baby carrying pouch for the bicycle. Trevor would strap the frame onto his back, put the child in it and ride off on his racing bicycle. It meant that William was almost ten feet off the ground. I was terrified for the child, but William loved the thrill. Trevor had great fun with William; all four of my children adored William; we still do even though he's a big strapping Garda of twenty-four now.

In December 1984 we moved to Naas, and Trevor went to the local secondary school to finish his education. Judy and Tootsie were in their late teens and going to discos in Rathcoole. I always picked them up at eleven o'clock, even if the disco went on until one o'clock in the morning. They could hear me coming up the drive in the old Mini with its dodgy exhaust pipe. It was like an early warning system. A friend would hear the car putt-putting up the drive and inform the girls, who would have to say a quick farewell to whichever boy they might be dancing with, so that, as I pulled up outside the venue, they would be just coming out the door to meet me.

I was always particular about picking up the kids from venues.

We had no public transport to speak of. If you needed to go some-where around Naas, you would either get a lift with someone you knew or hitch. I didn't encourage the kids to thumb lifts. Years before, I had thumbed a lift from the Green Isle Hotel at New-land's Cross on the outskirts of Dublin back to Saggart village where we lived. There weren't that many cars on the road in the early 1960s but this one man picked me up in his Morris Minor. I asked to be let out at Saggart, but he kept driving and continued on until Naas. It was very late and he took a turn down an empty road by Lawlor's Hotel and stopped. My door was locked from the inside, on some sort of a clip that I couldn't open. He went to maul me but I managed to get out past him through his door. Ironically, my only way home that night was to thumb another lift back to Saggart. It made me wary of hitching and when my kids were growing up I always told them to be wary of accepting lifts. If they really had to take a lift from someone, I suggested they could at least trust someone in uniform: the postman, a policeman or a sol-dier. 'These are good working people,' I said, 'and they can be easily identified.' These words were to come back to haunt me years later when the chief suspect in Trevor's murder was a high ranking soldier in the French army.

When Trevor was seventeen he was starting to go to discos, pri-marily to meet girls. It was coming up to exam time and he was doing the Leaving Cert. He started to leave for school really early in the morning, around 7am, saying that he was going to his friend's house, then onto school as they had to be in early for study. I found his behaviour a bit strange because Trevor hated getting up early. I was further puzzled because his friend's house was quite a distance in the opposite direction from our house and the school and it was unusual that they had been singled out to come to school so early when everyone else was expected at 9am. I became suspicious and thought, he can't like school that much. One morning, I followed him as he left our house. I held back a little so he wouldn't see me and watched as he went into a house not far from ours. I waited a short while, about ten minutes, and when he didn't emerge, I went to the door and knocked. A young girl answered the door. She was about seventeen, very pretty, and wearing a dressing gown. I asked her if Trevor was there. 'Yes,' she said, surprised. I asked her name and she told me. I then asked her who else was in the house. 'No one,' she replied, more hesitantly. Her mum had to leave the house at 6am to get into Dublin for a course and her father was dead. So my Trevor was making the most of the situation, disappearing every morning to visit this girl, when she wasn't even up and dressed! I forbade Trevor from leaving our house before a quarter to nine in the morning. That evening, I went to see the girl's mother and said I was barring Trevor from seeing her daughter. I said, 'If you want to be a grandmother, fine, but I don't.' Trevor called me 'an old hag' after my investigation. That was the worst insult he could ever think to say to me. If only he could see me now!

This episode didn't put the girls off him, nor him off them. There would always be girls coming round to the house, standing at the garden gate, waiting for him. He had been part-time bar-working since he was fifteen. It meant that he had no fear of talking to people and learnt to mix effortlessly with others. It was probably why the girls liked him; he could talk and socialise with ease. As he became more popular I grew more uneasy with all the attention he was drawing.

I was paranoid that any of my kids would 'get caught out' as I called it. I had always encouraged them to do well at school so they could get good jobs and be independent, not to get saddled with children too early. I was especially terrified that the girls would get pregnant and used to say I would put 'the pill' in their dinner. If I knew one of their schoolfriends had become pregnant, I'd say, 'Don't be going near that one.' Judy, exasperated, would retort, 'Mum, it's not the measles she's got.'

And as for the lads, I told them to respect girls. I'd tell them, 'Don't do to any girl what you wouldn't want done to your sister.'

I was very relieved when Trevor joined the FCA. I couldn't have been happier sending him off in the evenings to climb hills and go orienteering. Luckily, he loved it too. He called it the Free Clothing Association because he got boots and all the outdoor gear he would ever need. He was interested in pursuing a career in the military or the garda, in doing something physical that would challenge him and would ultimately be an adventure. Being healthy and fit was very important to him. He was always working out with his weights and had bought little lightweight ones to carry around.

It was now the mid 1980s and, as in so many Irish families then, my kids started to leave home and emigrate. It was the worst time. Over a period of eighteen months, three of my five kids left home to find work elsewhere. Judy was the first to go. She left school and went to New Zealand. The rest of us bawled, crying for weeks after she left. We couldn't believe she had gone and so far away. All of us missed her so much. It was like a death in the family.

Then, within a few short months, Tootsie went to England. She was going out with a soldier from Wexford and he decided to go to England with her. The relationship didn't last long, but Tootsie stayed in England. After James did his Leaving Cert he too went off to England, this time to college in Luton to do Engineering. During his holidays he would rent a rickshaw in London's China-town to make extra money to see him through college.

As much as I wanted them all to do well and be independent, I was devastated when they actually left. Now I only had Trevor and William at home. At five and half, William was at least a while off leaving home, but Trevor was nearly eighteen and it was only a matter of time before he too would follow the others on the road to God-knows-where. Already he was talking about joining the British Army. I wasn't happy with this at all but I knew where he got the idea.

When Trevor turned eighteen, in November, 1985, he decided he was a man and would go looking for his father, Jimmy O'Keeffe, from whom I had separated when he was three and who had gone back to England where he had been born. I felt that Trevor was making a big mistake. I had known Jimmy only too well. Trevor didn't know him at all. But I wouldn't stand in his way.

In the meantime he spent a year working around Naas, doing bar work. He was still keen to find his father, but, apart from that, he didn't really know what he wanted to do with his life and was still toying with the idea of joining the British Army.

When he was growing up, Trevor used to say that someday he would be rich and famous. I don't know where he got this idea from, probably television, but he was convinced of it. He decided that when he went to England, his life and future would all fall into place. He thought it would be a great adventure, to find his dad, be mates with him and start a new life with him. But it didn't work out that way.

At the beginning of summer 1987, Trevor made his way to Jimmy's house in St Albans, outside London. He stayed with him for a few weeks but very quickly realised that he actually didn't like Jimmy. He was devastated. His feelings, his plans, his future all seemed awry. He plunged into a real crisis and didn't know what to do. He couldn't understand why he didn't get on with his own father. I wasn't surprised, but I was hurt that Trevor felt it so badly.

Jimmy had left the family in 1970, but when I asked for a separation, ten years later, he would only agree if I gave him money to go away. I had been working in various jobs over the years to buy the house we lived in in Saggart from the Council. I paid off the house, sold it, and with the proceeds was able to pay Jimmy £3,000. I also agreed that I wouldn't come after him for support or maintenance for the children. I then took a job managing a pub in Mullingar, which had living accommodation overhead. The whole family moved down; Judy was sixteen at the time, and Trevor was only twelve. I put them all in new schools in Mullingar. We lived there for three years before moving to Naas. It would take until 1984 before I could get back on my feet financially and otherwise. I was angry with Jimmy and I suppose I made it worse by telling Trevor that I felt his father had 'sold' the four of them for £3,000.

Now, in the summer of 1987, Trevor didn't know what to do, where to go. After leaving his father's house, he went into digs and Tootsie got him bar work in St Albans, but things weren't working out as he had planned at all. I hoped that when he came home from England we could talk things out, work out what he wanted to do in the future. I told him it would be fine, he would be fine and he and I would work it out together, like we always did. But in the meantime he decided to go off to France with his young work colleague, Christian Jaillet. Perhaps it was because he was in such an unsettled frame of mind that he decided to go to France.

So, when it came down to it, I blamed myself for him going to France, even though I knew that he had to make his own way in life and learn the truth about his father for himself. But he was angry, really upset and I felt I'd let him down, by marrying the wrong man, by not being a good enough mother, by trying to bring him up without any Dad for so many years, by not encouraging him to see his own father earlier. Whatever it was, I knew it was my fault.

CHAPTER 3

Why is No One Doing Anything?

I tried to keep it a secret that my son was murdered. I didn't want anyone to know what had happened because I felt it was my fault. I felt such great shame that I could not take care of my own son. How could I call myself a mother and let my son be murdered, and so horrifically? I also felt enormous guilt because of the way I had left things with Trevor before he went to France. I felt that everything that had happened to him was my fault, and my failure. Then I pretended he wasn't dead, that we hadn't buried him at all.

Sometimes I would be going to town in Naas for shopping and I couldn't stop for fear of someone saying anything about Trevor to me. One evening one of my neighbours met me as I was rounding up William for his tea. She said, 'I am sorry about Trevor'. But I just said, 'Trevor is fine, so what?' I didn't know this woman, but she had sons, one of whom knew Trevor well.

I would not admit to anyone that Trevor was dead. I really tried to keep it a secret because of how he died. How stupid of me. Dead is dead. Nothing can change it or the horror of it. I did not want to admit that some awful, cruel person deliberately murdered my beautiful son, and even now, after all these years, I still find it hard to believe. Time means nothing. Trevor is dead forever. But he left his mark on all of us who loved him, so he will never be forgotten.

I only really started crying after the funeral; crying and not letting my family know. I told my girls, 'don't cry' and all the time I was crying in my sleep. I would wake up crying and pray that Trevor was alive and that it was only a dream. Next day I would hide in the wardrobe and cry when my children were downstairs and thought I had gone out.

I couldn't bring myself to tell William that his beloved brother was dead. We all tried to keep it from him since he was so little. In the first few days it wasn't too difficult, because a good friend of mine, Jane McCoy, took him in and looked after him. She had two sons of similar age to William and sent them all to school every morning. Even on the day of the funeral I sent William to school and Jane picked him up and kept him that night. But she couldn't keep him forever and of course we had to have him home with us. I felt he wouldn't have understood what was going on and I didn't want him to see the trauma of what the rest of us were going through. But he did see it and he listened and heard everything that was going on. He told me all this years later, but I think I already knew it at the time. We were all so distraught, we couldn't hide it, but we pretended to him that we were fine and to ourselves that he believed us.

I was trying to run the household as normal, sparing the family the gory details of Trevor's murder. I didn't know that much about his death but I knew enough that I had to protect my four remaining kids from it. How could they have coped if they knew all the details? Sometimes I'm glad even now that I didn't know exactly how he died in those early days. It was enough to try and deal with the fact that he was dead, let alone, as I found out a decade later, that he was probably abused before he died.

In the days, weeks and months that followed Trevor's death, no one in our house could even mention Trevor's name without turning to tears. The grief was relentless. One minute you could be having a conversation about nothing too important; it could be what was for dinner or who had left the light on in the upstairs landing last night, and some tiny thing would remind you of Trevor, of something he would have said or done, something seemingly unconnected, and you would have to sit down with the weight of crying. It didn't seem to stop.

During the time we were waiting for Trevor to come home, the kids all went out and got jobs to keep going. I suppose they needed them simply to keep functioning. Tootsie was in Superquinn supermarket, Judy went up to Dublin and got a job in The Royal Bank of Scotland on Saint Stephen's Green, and James was working in a bar.

I took so much time off work from Atlantic Homecare. I never told them the real reason. In the end I left the job and Noeleen gave me work in the kitchen of her nursing home, so I could at least have some money coming into the house. It was primarily an act of charity on her part as I wasn't great in the kitchen or serving to the clients. Often it was a case of 'Do you want to eat your dinner or wear it?' Still, Noeleen was as patient with me as she was with her charges.

At night I would get into the car and drive up the Kilcullen Road, near our home, as late as eleven or twelve o'clock, just to cry, so my family would not know, to try and spare them my grief. One Friday evening in October, in the dark and pouring rain, I walked the few miles from my house to Pat Donlea's garage in Kilcullen and turned back, hoping a car would run me over and kill me, to spare me the horror of losing Trevor, and so my children would not blame me for his death. When they had learned about Trevor's plans to reunite with Jimmy, some of them had tried to warn him as to what their Dad was really like, but still it was me who had made the mistake of actually marrying the man in the first place. So it was my fault.

Cars blew their horns at me. A police car stopped me and asked me where I was going. I said I had just come out for a walk. They offered me a lift, but I said, 'I'm fine. I am entitled to walk.' They said it wasn't safe. I told them, 'I am OK, thank you. I'll be fine.' And I was, that night.

I tried repeatedly to contact the Jaillet family in Poligny, and in particular their son, Christian, both through the police in Saint-Quentin and through Tootsie and her friends in England who had worked with Christian in the pub. The family had never got in touch with me, even after Trevor's body had been identified and the newspapers in France carried the story. I wanted so desperately to know how he had been when he left them. So many questions haunted me. Who would have last seen Trevor, who talked to him last? I found out from the police that Christian had been questioned after the body was found, but was immediately eliminated from their enquiries.

In my own head I had a new suspect in Trevor's murder every day: people he knew or had met on his travels; did someone follow him from England, did he have enemies here at home? I would lie awake some nights and try to piece together what had happened Trevor. Who would have killed him and how? I had so little to go on; nothing really, except my own wild imagination.

Eventually the kids all had to leave and go back to their 'real' jobs and somehow return to the lives they had before Trevor was murdered. Judy went back to New Zealand and Tootsie to St Albans. James went to France to stay with Caroline for two months, and then also headed back to St Albans.

I was left with William and Bill. I returned Noeleen's kindness by leaving her kitchen and getting a job of my own. I got myself a taxi licence and started driving for a living. I was working nights so that I could be around for William when he got home from school. Sometimes, though, my mind would be elsewhere and I was for-getful. I left William to school one day and returned home. The next thing, William turned up at the front door. Another mother had brought him home. It was a holiday and I'd completely forgot-ten that the school would be closed. Another time I went to the garage shop to get a newspaper and got back into the car and drove off, leaving him on the forecourt. He laughs about it now and reminds me how I went off and left him. I was in a daze and it lasted longer than I have ever admitted. I am overwhelmed with grief even now when I think of Trevor and what happened to him, or rather what probably happened, because I'll never know for sure what torture he did go through before he was murdered. But worse than the grief is the fact that I wasn't there when he needed me most.

I would drive through Naas, see one of Trevor's friends and say to myself, 'Trevor is alive; he is not dead. You are not dead. Be home when I come home, Trevor, or I will kill you for making us go through all this! See you later, you little brat. Have the fire light-ing for me and the house warm.'

For months and years afterwards, I kept Trevor's room just as it was when he left. For fourteen years I slept with his pyjamas under my pillow and hugged them close, in case, by morning, he might materialise into them and be home with me, my little son, my boy. I wouldn't even wash them. I pretended he was still alive. I would even put a dinner on for him in the evenings, always cook enough so that if he came in he could eat with us.

I would wash his clothes as if he were still at home and wearing them during the week. They would be washed, ironed and waiting for him in the press or his room.

How long did this go for? I don't know. Am I over his death even now? No, I don't think so. I remember Tootsie was home one year and making up my bed and she came down the stairs, crying. She was holding Trevor's pyjamas in her hand. 'What were these doing under your pillow, Mum, after all these years?' I don't think our family will ever be the same again, no matter how long Trevor is gone from us.

There were just weeks and months of helplessness, of not knowing what to do or who to talk to. The situation was made more insurmountable by the language barrier. I couldn't speak a word of French, so I couldn't even pick up the phone to Captain Skoczylas and ask, 'well, is there any news?' It was so basic, not being able to communicate. I felt so useless.

Instead I made calls to my solicitor and to Foreign Affairs, and I had Caroline in France also trying to find out what information she could. I now feel really bad about Caroline and how much translation she had to do of such awful information, including the early newspaper reports of how Trevor was found. She was only a young woman at the time, barely into her early twenties, not much older than Trevor, and a slip of a girl, really. I know she didn't mind, but it seemed a big burden for someone so young.

As the days turned into months, any official information dried up and it was as if the whole investigation had come to a standstill. I had got my son home and had buried him and I felt that the authorities expected me to be content that that was the end of the affair. There never seemed to be any news from France as to whether anyone was being questioned for the murder, who was investigating it, what clues had they found. Nothing.

Caroline would send over any newspaper articles she could find relating to Trevor's murder and the inquiry. Also, when Noeleen and I were in France to identify the body, and again when we brought Trevor home, we bought newspapers every day to check for any information relating to his murder. We scoured the pages of whatever newspapers we could find in Saint-Quentin for any mention of Trevor O'Keeffe. I looked for words I might recognise: 'Alaincourt', the place where Trevor's body was discovered, and 'Irlandais'. I became familiar with the French words for victim, autopsy, dead body, strangled.

Back home in Naas, I had to find someone to translate the little articles I found. One local woman volunteered and translated some articles in the days and months after Trevor's body was found. She wrote out the translations by hand. Then one day she called to say she couldn't continue; she found it all too distressing. I felt really bad about having inflicted that on her.

When I had gone to Saint-Quentin to bring Trevor home, I gave Captain Skoczylas photographs of Trevor, including the ones we had taken before he left for England with his new rucksack and clothes. He promised me he would notify all the surrounding police stations of Trevor's murder and would distribute Trevor's photos to try and find out if anyone had seen him hitchhiking or had given him a lift. I believed him when he said he would do this. I really had no choice.

I later discovered that the only knowledge of Trevor's murder that ever made it to the public were a few small pieces in the local paper of Saint-Quentin, saying that the body of the man had been identified as Trevor O'Keeffe, from Naas, Ireland and calling for witnesses to come forward; nothing more. I had trusted the police, believed them when they said they would do all they could to find and prosecute Trevor's killer without delay. I never, for one moment, thought that sixteen years later I would still be going back to France to find out who had killed my son.

The Irish newspapers picked up on the story on and off over the years. In the beginning, they published all manner of wrong and half-wrong information about the case, from reporting that Trevor had been killed in Brittany and that police were holding two suspects, to horrifically detailed reports of how Trevor had been found, claiming that he was naked.

Noeleen would ring me to say that a particular paper was carrying a report. I would go into four different shops so as not to look strange buying bulk copies and buy four copies – one for me, and one to send to each of the older kids. I particularly didn't want to alert people to the fact that my family and I were mentioned in the paper. However I would read the article and invariably it would have some gory detail in it that I felt would be too traumatic to read, so I would decide then that none of my kids actually needed to see it at all.

I had to protect them at all costs, so it was easier for me to just keep the papers myself. As the years passed, I amassed stacks of multiple copies of newspapers and photocopies that I then stashed in pillowcases and suitcases and stuffed into the bottom of wardrobes, hidden out of sight of everybody. The one thing I couldn't do was to throw them out.

I called my lawyer in Dublin, Garret Sheehan, every week to find out if he had been talking to Antoine Comte in Paris and if there was any news. There never was.

I needed to do something. I started to write to various people I thought might be able to help: local politicians, followed by national politicians. Over the next months, then years, and then a decade, I sent letters to Alan Dukes TD, Gerard Collins, who was Minister for Foreign Affairs, then later Dick Spring when he was Tánaiste and Minister for Foreign Affairs; to Mary Banotti, MEP and to President Mary Robinson. I wrote lots of letters to anybody and everybody I could think of who might be able to help get Trevor's case moving.

I even wrote to the media and newspaper tycoon, Robert Maxwell, because I had seen an article in one of his newspapers about someone else who had just been murdered in France. I thought he might be able to help. He didn't answer me but I did get a nice letter back from Paul Foot, the editor of the newspaper. I got lots of letters, all similar replies of sympathetic regret, but nothing that could offer me any help. It seemed that nobody could do anything to help me.

One day in December 1987, a very different letter arrived. It was not addressed to me but addressed to Trevor. The envelope was postmarked France. I could barely open it for shock. My hands shaking, I unfolded it. The letter read:

Hello!

My name is Joëlle Charuel ...

Please, everyone you are, can you write to me to tell me if Trevor Charles Matthew O'Keeffe always live here and if he is safe.

Because in the forest near our house, we've found a tent and a camping bag with papers.

This papers are a birth certificate of Trevor Charles Matthew O'Keeffe, some employ certificates and a certificate of discharge.

Please can you write to us to tell news of Trevor because we worry about him.

Thanks a lot and I hope to have an answer quickly.

Mme Charuel.

I held the letter in my hand for a long time. I didn't know what to do with it. I felt sick. For a mere split second before I read it I had thought, hoped, believed it was from Trevor, telling me everything was OK and he had found a job and was coming home. And now, as I held this piece of paper in my hand, I knew Trevor would not be coming home and it was just another day devastated by the loss of him.

Later I did respond to Joëlle, and in fact, eighteen years on, we are still in touch. As one mother to another, she had been worried for the boy whose rucksack and papers she had found. And I am eternally grateful to her for that. Her letter was also a turning point for me for lots of reasons, not least because of her humanity, but also because of what it revealed about the investigation into my son's murder. It was only when I had read it, and subsequently understood the background to Joëlle's discovery and dealings with the police, that I finally knew what I needed to do.

One evening in the middle of August 1987, Joëlle's husband, Thierry, had found a rucksack while out walking near their camping ground on Lac Du Der, a scenic area around a huge reservoir south of Saint-Quentin and near the army base of Mourmelon. It was an area where people went to cut wood in the same way Irish people might cut turf. It was situated almost halfway between Poligny, where Trevor had been staying with his friend's family, and Alaincourt, where his body was found. Scattered nearby were papers that had been in the rucksack, including Trevor's birth certificate and his discharge letter from the FCA.

Suspecting that the rucksack had been stolen, the Charuels immediately contacted their local police who, over the phone, nonchalantly told them to hang on to it themselves in case someone came looking for it. Reluctantly, the Charuels hung the rucksack, with its contents, up on a nail in their garage. The rucksack was still hanging on its nail some months later when Joëlle decided to take the matter into her own hands and write to the address she found in the personal papers, thinking that the person who had lost the papers might be relieved to know they were safe and could reclaim them.

I took the letter to Naas Garda station and gave them the number and contact of the station in Saint-Quentin where the investigation was ongoing. The Gardaí sent the letter to the French police. Soon afterwards Joëlle was surprised by a large contingent of local police and police from Paris who came to take away the rucksack and papers. Only then did the police tell her what had happened to Trevor. She was stunned. She had no idea when she wrote the letter to Trevor that he had been murdered such a short time before her husband had found the rucksack and belongings. And she was also shocked to realise that for over four months she had such crucial evidence hanging up on a nail in her garage.

The police asked Joëlle's husband to sign a document saying that they – the police – had done their work correctly. Joëlle's husband refused to sign the document and the police were not happy. They argued amongst themselves, but in the end they had to leave with the rucksack and evidence but no signed documentation as to how appropriately they had carried out their job.

Many years later, I found out that the chief suspect in Trevor's murder, Pierre Chanal, had been in Lac Du Der at the same time as Thierry Charuel found the rucksack; he was doing parachute jumps in the local parachute club. I also discovered that among Trevor's possessions there had been an itinerary of his journey home, with a list of the towns he would need to hitch through.

What Joëlle's letter and subsequent correspondence confirmed to me was the shocking revelation that the authorities were not doing their job properly. I felt so stupid. I had been sitting on my laurels, waiting for the police to contact me, which they had not done, despite this crucial find. Questions started to race through my head. Why were my son's belongings found so far away from where his body was located? Had he actually been killed at Lac Du Der? How long had the rucksack and papers been lying there before the Charuels found them? Had they been tested for fingerprints? Why had the local police not come out to investigate the rucksack, especially if, as Captain Skoczylas had promised, details of Trevor's murder, including

Above: Myself and the children at Tootsie's First Communion. (l to r): Judy, James, Trevor, Tootsie.

Below: A school photo of the children in 1975. (l to r): Judy (11), James (standing, 9), Trevor (8), Tootsie (10).

Above: A proud member of the primary school football team, Saggart. Trevor is second from right, front row.

Below: My little scamp. Trevor, aged eight.

Left: Trevor in the garden in Saggart, aged ten.

Right: Judy and Trevor having fun in a photo booth.

Above: The last photo I took of Trevor before he left for England in 1987. The socks are the same as those he was wearing when his body was discovered.

Right: Trevor with the rucksack, tent, new Walkman and beanie hat that he had acquired for his hitchhiking trip.

Hello!

My name is Joëlle Charuel. I live in France and here is my address.

Mrs Joëlle Charuel

Please, everyone you are, can you write to me to tell me if Trevor Charles Matthew O'Keeffe always live here and if he is safe.

Because in the forest near our house, we've found a tent and a camping bag with papers.

This papers are a birth certificate of Trevor Charles Matthew O'Keeffe, some employ certificates and a certificate of discharge.

Please can you write to us to tell news of Trevor because we worry about him.

Thanks a lot and I hope to have an answer quickly.

M.me Charuel

Above: The letter from Joëlle Charuel, received in December 1987, four months after Trevor was murdered. The Charuels had found Trevor's rucksack and papers and were worried about him.

Above: Michel Lente at the spot in Les Sablonnières, near Alaincourt, where he discovered Trevor's body. To the left of the photo is Jean Du Pont, who did so much to link Pierre Chanal to the murder of Trevor and the disappearance of the other young men.

Below: Thierry Charuel points to the location in Lac du Der where he found Trevor's rucksack and papers.

Above: French police working at the site where Trevor's body was discovered.

Bottom: Trevor's empty grave in the paupers' section of La Tombelle cemetery on the day of his exhumation.

the picture of him with the rucksack on his back, had been circulated to all police stations in France?

Joëlle's intervention as a concerned mother would be my turning point. When the police told her what had happened to Trevor, she wrote back to me:

I'm very sad for what happened to you. I have three sons and I know life would not be the same anymore if one of them was dead.

You must find the person who did this horrible crime.

I knew what I needed to do. There was nothing else for it. I had to accept that Trevor was dead, that he wouldn't be coming home to me. And I would have to find out who killed my son for myself.

CHAPTER 4

In Search of a Killer

Noeleen's daughter, Caroline, was our eyes and ears in France. Any information she could glean, from whatever source, that might have anything to do with Trevor, she passed on to us: she would send cuttings from newspapers, or phone with some piece of information she had picked up from television. While I could always call Caroline to ask her what was in the article, more generally I had to look for someone locally in Naas to translate the article. Getting translation done was a constant headache. As well as not knowing very many people who had fluent French, I was also paranoid about people from the town knowing all my business. My solution was to ask a range of people for help. In this way I had a number of people working on bits of documentation all over Naas, but at least I felt that the information any one person would be party to would be limited.

In January 1988, Caroline sent a newspaper cutting that profoundly unsettled Noeleen and myself. It reported that police were comparing Trevor's murder with the disappearances of a number of young men in an area known as 'The Triangle of Death'. This was a 15km area to the northeast of Paris, between the garrison town of Mourmelon, Châlons-sur-Marne and Mially-le-Camp, from where young men had been disappearing as far back as 1980. One body had been found in 1982 and it was suspected that the others had met a similar fate. At the centre of the 'Triangle of Death' was the army base in Mourmelon, the biggest in France and about the size of the Curragh military camp in Kildare. Six of the seven young men who had disappeared were conscripts in the army.

Trevor's hitchhiking route home was to travel to the port of Calais via Dijon, Vitry-le-François, Châlons-sur-Marne, Reims and Saint-Quentin. Unwittingly, he would have been travelling through this 'Triangle of Death'. Trevor's body had been found in Alaincourt, near Saint-Quentin, but his rucksack was discovered in Lac Du Der, a huge reservoir edged with flat countryside and woods and not far from Vitry-le-François. Between both locations was the army base of Mourmelon. Was Trevor murdered in the 'Triangle of Death' and if so, was it an isolated incident or the work of a serial killer?

We couldn't understand why the police had not mentioned anything about Mourmelon or the 'Triangle of Death' to us when we first met them, especially since young men had been going missing in the area for seven years before Trevor's death.

In March 1989, Caroline sent another article that made us even more suspicious. It was about a parachute trainer with the French Army who had been found with a young Hungarian student tied up in his van and whom he had abused for twenty hours. The soldier, Pierre Chanal, was an adjutant-chef in the French Army, the equivalent of a sergeant-major, and a former SAS commando. By pure chance, the police had stopped Chanal on a deserted country road at Bussières, in the Beaujolais region near Macon, southeast of Paris, and heard moaning coming from under a blanket inside the vehicle. On opening up the camping van, they discovered a young man from Hungary, a hitchhiker called Palazs Falvay, who had been picked up on the road by Chanal, abducted, then tied up and abused. Chanal even had a videotape of the assault in the van, along with other videotapes. Chanal was arrested for kidnapping, assault and sexual abuse of the hitchhiker.

In the newspaper articles that followed the arrest, Trevor's name was mentioned alongside this young Hungarian's. Apparently, the soldier, Pierre Chanal, had been stationed for many years at Mourmelon barracks, but for some reason had been transferred to another barracks at Fontainebleau, south of Paris. Had Trevor also taken a lift with Pierre Chanal? Worse still, did Chanal abuse Trevor in the same way as he did the Hungarian boy? Did Pierre Chanal murder Trevor?

When I met the French police in the first month or so after Trevor's death, they had told me that Trevor died quickly and never mentioned if he had been abused. Now I wondered whether they were holding back, trying to spare me a more awful truth. I couldn't bear to think of my son being hurt in any way but I needed to know what had happened to him.

A third article sent by Caroline was about an organisation called *Les Disparus de Mourmelon* (The Disappeared of Mourmelon) which was set up by the parents of the young conscripts who had disappeared from the Mourmelon army base. The army had maintained that the young recruits had deserted. They scoffed at any suggestion that there might be a more sinister reason for the disappearances. However, the conscripts' parents did not agree and wanted answers, especially in the light of Chanal's arrest. Four of the young recruits had served under Chanal at Mourmelon. In fact, throughout the 1980s, the military, including Chanal, had been warning young conscripts leaving the base at weekends not to hitchhike alone.

All of this information had come, not from the police or French authorities, but from newspaper reports. Despite my constant calls, I could get nothing from the investigators myself. I felt I was getting nowhere.

In September 1988, I wrote to Garret Sheehan who then wrote to Antoine Comte in Paris. I asked them what could I do, given that Trevor's name was being connected in the media with this man Chanal? Antoine Comte suggested two possible courses of action. One was to take a civil action in the course of the criminal inquiry, to allow one to become '*partie civile*' to the inquiry and thus be informed of anything new concerning Trevor. I was not fully aware of what this action meant and it would actually be 1994 before I got access to the documents from the criminal inquiry. Secondly, he suggested I make an immediate claim for compensation for Trevor from the French and Irish authorities, despite there not being a formal reciprocal agreement between them, since this action would be independent of the criminal inquiry. What this meant in real terms was that any work the lawyer could do in the short-term would be related to the compensation case and we had to wait and see if the investigators could uncover evidence to charge Chanal with Trevor's murder.

I couldn't wait that long. This man Chanal could be my son's murderer. I needed to act now.

Noeleen and I organised flights to Paris. When I look back on it now, we were like two women possessed. We hadn't a clue really what we were doing, but we were driven by an overwhelming urge to find out what had happened to Trevor, and more importantly, to find the person responsible for his death. We were doing it for Trevor. I desperately needed to know who killed him, and how, especially since I felt the police were not interested in the case and that there was more to it than they were telling me. Noeleen was there to make sure I didn't do anything stupid. She was the typical big sister and, I have to admit, she had a point. As well as having written letters to various politicians I had also, on occasion, camped outside their houses. I door-stepped both Dick Spring and Emmet Stagg when they were ministers, to petition them to help me get some answers on my son's case. I was frantic for information and I didn't really care how I got it.

When we got to France, we were going to meet up with Caroline and with Noeleen's son, David, who was only sixteen at the time, and who spent his summer holidays in France. We would take him with us because he had picked up the language pretty well while he was there and was studying French at school; we thought he could translate for us. Looking back, it was something of a desperate measure, but we knew so few people with any working knowledge of the language that we didn't have much choice.

I decided to get us off to a head start by buying phonecards on the flight that would see us through the trip. But without a knowledge of French even the most simple of tasks was never straightforward for us.

When we touched down in Paris, I tried to call Caroline, using one of the cards. Not only did I have to ring one number to decode the card but then I'd have to call another number in order to use the card, by which time the first card had run out and I had to do the whole palaver again with the next card. There was probably an easier way to make the card work. Standing outside the phone box, surrounded by luggage, a chilly Noeleen was not amused. 'Why can't you just use money, like anybody else?' she huffed 'Why buy the thing if you don't know how to use it?'

'I do know how to use it,' I said defensively, 'I'm just getting the numbers now. Bear with me.' In the end I had to abandon both card and phone box.

We got the train to Caroline's house. The atmosphere inside the carriage was almost as frosty as it was outside. Luckily, Noeleen had thawed out by the time we got to her daughter's house and was talking to me again. From there, Caroline drove us to Saint-Quentin. It was late. We had booked ourselves into Hotel de Guise, the same hotel we'd stayed in when we first went to France. Caroline had bought David a bicycle and nothing would do him but to bring it all the way to Saint-Quentin with us, strapped to the car. We got the last room in the place, at the very top of the building and David had to struggle with the new bike all the way up a flight of narrow stairs to the room. We all piled into the one room: myself, Noeleen, David and Caroline. 'Now,' I said to David, commandeering his new bicycle as a room divider, 'you don't be looking at us old ones!' I got a sheet and threw it over the bicycle that I had placed between our beds and David's bed. The boy was mortified.

The next morning, we got up early and had a quick breakfast before driving over to the police station. David said he would go on his new bicycle. We arrived at the police station and waited for him. We wouldn't go inside until he arrived. Time passed and still there was no sign of him. As we waited, our agitation turned to genuine anxiety. In ordinary circumstances we probably wouldn't have given David's lateness a second thought; he was obviously lost and would find us eventually, but these were no ordinary circumstances and we had already lost one son in France. An hour later David turned up, to receive a ferocious three-headed dressing-down, albeit from his mostly relieved mother, aunt and sister.

Once inside the police station, we began to go through the list of questions we had prepared. Top of the list was about the organisation called 'The Disappeared of Mourmelon'. We wanted to know who they were and how we could get in touch with them. We asked what did the police know of the young men who had disappeared, and who were suspected of having been killed? What was being done to seek out the perpetrators? We wanted to know was there a connection between the disappearance of these young men and Trevor's murder? We may as well have been talking to the wall for all the response we got. The police told us there was no organisation called 'The Disappeared of Mourmelon', but Caroline argued with them that there was. Before our meeting with the police, I had called Foreign Affairs about it, but they also had never heard of the organisation. I felt like we'd hit a dead end. We decided on another avenue. We would go back to where Trevor's body was found and start our investigation from there.

On our first visit to France, on the day that we went to the cemetery to see where the police had buried Trevor, we had met with Michel Lente, the farmer who had found Trevor's body. I had been so grateful that he had discovered Trevor's body. However, on that occasion, because of the language difficulty, I had not been able to speak to Michel properly or ask any questions about the state in which he found Trevor. The two policemen who had accompanied us didn't have enough English to translate for me. This time, however, I had come prepared, or as prepared as I could be. Caroline and David would translate for me.

Off we went in search of Michel's house. We headed for the locale where Trevor was found, called Les Sablonnières, near Alaincourt, just off the A26 north/south autoroute – a main arterial road running north/south through France. The last time we'd been on this road, I had been struck by how featureless and indistinguishable the landscape was. However, on this trip I noticed that there were some houses, but was delighted that there were so few. Hopefully, this would mean that our search for Michel would not take long. It was a small community, very rural and not even big enough to be called a village. The houses were quite scattered and the area was very flat, with poplar trees lining the edges of fields. We stopped and called to a few doors and were further heartened as everyone seemed to know everyone else. Our quest was soon resolved. We were directed to Michel's house and he kindly invited us in.

Caroline did all the talking. She spoke like a real French person would: rapid-fire delivery and big passionate hand gestures. She and Michel quickly became immersed in animated conversation, she asking question after question, to which he gave long expressive answers. What was he saying? It was so frustrating not being able to follow the conversation. I had to keep stopping Caroline mid-flow: 'Caroline, speak English, tell us what he said.' It probably looked quite comical, really. Sometimes she didn't have the right word in English and she'd be thinking out loud as to what the word was, waving her arms about in frustration. David tried to help but myself and Noeleen could do nothing more than simply stare blankly back at her.

The conversation carried on for hours and eventually I felt more content with what I was hearing. What also became very clear as our discussion went on was how much Michel had been affected by finding Trevor's body. He was angry that someone could commit such a crime on a defenceless young man. I felt he was part of our campaign. He wanted to find the killer as much as we did. We were in this together.

Later, Michel took us to the place where he had found Trevor, to show us exactly how he found him. He shook his head in sorrow as he told us all the details of how he had found him. It was around 8.30pm on Saturday, 8 August, 1987, and he was out with his gun and his dog. He was a keen hunter and knew the countryside well. As he walked along, he noticed something odd at the side of the road. Branches had been broken and nettles had been flattened, making a track down a slope. The dog went down first and Michel followed him into the hollow and what was an old bomb crater. He noticed a suspicious looking mound covered by a thin layer of soil. He thought perhaps someone had buried an animal there. He broke a branch off one of the trees and carefully raked away some soil. He saw a hand. He went back up the gulley to the road to get help and alert the police. He later learned that the body was Trevor's and that he had been strangled.

Michel had his own ideas as to Trevor's murderer. He told us that he thought Trevor had been a soldier because he'd heard of young conscripts who had disappeared from the army base at Mourmelon. It seemed that everyone in the area knew about 'The Disappeared'. There had to be a connection.

For many years afterwards, whenever myself and Noeleen went to France, we would always make time to go up to Les Sablonnières, to the place where Trevor was found. I had a need to talk to Michel Lente, again and again. I don't know if I was looking for new clues or simple comfort. He was always welcoming and always keen to update us on anything that might have relevance to the case. On one occasion he introduced us to a neighbour of his who came to meet us in a very excited manner. She told us what she had told the police: that she had seen a green van, like Pierre Chanal's, in the area a week before Trevor's body was found. We thought that this was very relevant information, but the police chose not to use her testimony as evidence.

Through researching newspaper articles and talking to people, Caroline had found a name relating to 'The Disappeared of Mourmelon'. It was Madame Havet, whose son, Serge, an army conscript, had disappeared on 20 February 1981. She had helped set up the organisation, which represented the families of the other young conscripts who had disappeared. The bodies of these young conscripts, bar one, had never been recovered. This was to have a major impact on the case against Chanal many years later. But, while Caroline had a name, she didn't know where the woman lived, and there was no phone number or any way of contacting her. Again we had hit another dead end.

After a few days of fruitless and expensive searching, we went home to Kildare. From now on we would have to save both information and money if we wanted to pursue our investigations in France. While the taxi I had was flexible enough in terms of the hours I could work, it wasn't as reliable financially as I would have liked. I felt I had to find another job, one that would pay better but still give me good flexibility in terms of taking time off. I started to look at my options.

Meanwhile, Caroline sent us more articles from newspapers. The media in France continued to link Pierre Chanal's abduction of the young Hungarian hitchhiker with the death of another young hitchhiker, my son Trevor. Newspapers in Ireland began picking up on the story about the 'Rambo-Sadist' Pierre Chanal and his link with Trevor's death. While I was getting nowhere with the French authorities, I went back to Antoine Comte in Paris, through Garrett Sheehan in Dublin, to ask if there was anything new in Trevor's case and if I could now bring civil proceedings against Chanal, who was then in custody. In January 1989 I received confirmation from Garrett Sheehan that they had instructed solicitors in Paris to take proceedings on my behalf. I believed that Chanal had something to do with Trevor's murder, but didn't know at the time that Chanal had already been questioned about his murder; it would be a further five years before I was privy to this particular information. In the meantime I was given no information at all as to Chanal's possible connection with my son's death.

From my home in Naas, I felt I was being passed from Billy to Jack right from the start of the whole process. In official telephone calls and communications, I was transferred from Foreign Affairs to various other ministries. No one explained the French process to me. I had no idea how any of it worked. Myself and Noeleen were in the dark.

While we were told who the investigating magistrate was, we were never told what he did. We had no idea how he related to the case but we had to make an appointment to see him. We did this through Foreign Affairs. The judge in question was Judge Charles Marien. He was the fourth judge to deal with Trevor's file. The other three had passed us by since we had no understanding of the system and what to do. What we didn't know at the time was that Trevor's case had, in fact, been added to those of the 'Disappeared', and because these had occurred in different areas, the files had been passed around various investigating magistrates, from Amiens to Reims, to Saint-Quentin. We only became aware of this at our first meeting with Judge Marien, which didn't take place until 1994.

Caroline called us with news on 23 October 1990. Pierre Chanal had been sentenced to ten years in prison for rape, indecent assault and abduction of Palazs Falvay at the court of Assizes in the town of Saone-et-Loire. We were aware that the trial would be happening but didn't know when or where, so hadn't followed it on a day-to-day basis. It was not until the sentence was handed down that the media could openly speculate on the connection between Chanal and the 'Disappeared of Mourmelon' without it being prejudicial to the case. We wondered what effect the Chanal verdict might have on Trevor's case; surely it would make it more likely that Chanal had been involved in his murder if he had been convicted of the abduction of another young man?

In the wake of his conviction, there was a flurry of newspaper articles about Chanal. Two pieces of information that cropped up in several of the articles almost leapt off the page to me. One was that his Volkswagen van had yielded loads of clues, including a number of men's underpants and lots of different hair samples, suggesting that the young Hungarian had not been the only person to have been held in that vehicle. The second was that Chanal's room at his barracks in Fontainebleau, south of Paris, had been made available to the police since his arrest. Were there similar clues to be found there?

Back during that awful first visit to Saint-Quentin police station in 1987, the police had shown me photographs of Trevor's body wearing the clothes in which he was found. They included his jeans, his running shoes (one of which was removed), a shirt, socks and his watch. Later I would discover that he had been wearing French-made underpants that were not his size, which raised further questions about the possibility of an assault, but no mention was made of this at the time.

Later, when police recovered Trevor's rucksack from Lac Du Der, only personal papers, including his birth certificate and discharge papers from the FCA, were discovered inside. Where were all the rest of his clothes? Had they been dumped along the road or could they have been hoarded by someone, stored at home by the person who killed him, for example?

There were two places I thought Trevor's belongings might be found and I asked the French authorities in Saint-Quentin repeatedly to allow me to see them. I wanted to see the contents of Chanal's van and his room at the barracks. I instinctively felt I had a right to view those for myself because if there was something of Trevor's there, I would be able to recognise it immediately and so tie Chanal to Trevor's murder. I made my first request to Judge Marien in 1989 and for the next few years I would repeat this request with a polite letter: 'May I see the contents of Chanal's van, please? May I see the contents of Chanal's quarters in the barracks, please?' I received no reply.

Finally, in 1991, Judge Marien sent a letter asking me to make a list of everything Trevor had in his possession going to France.

This was the first time I'd been requested to make such a list, four years after Trevor's death, and more importantly for the case, four years after his belongings had been found in Lac Du Der.

I was keen to remember as much as I could. I made a list of everything he had taken with him to England at the beginning of the summer, both what he had bought himself and what I had bought for him. Tootsie had seen Trevor off from St Albans to France that summer so she set about making a list of everything she remembered him packing for the trip. We decided to cross-reference our lists so that we wouldn't leave anything out. As we each set about the task, I felt, for the first time in a long time, that at last I was finally doing something useful. The case was moving.

Between Tootsie and myself, we came up with everything we could, which included a pair of sunglasses and the new Walkman, both of which had never been recovered. The list of his clothes was long; it included a yellow cardigan, black jeans and blue jeans, white, blue and grey shirts, a grey suit, a black dicky-bow for work in the bar, T-shirts in a variety of colours, denim shirts in blue and black, a Hawaiian shirt that was all the fashion then, a Nottingham Forest T-shirt, an Irish harp T-shirt, multi-coloured Bermuda shorts – they looked huge on him but he loved them – white trainers, black shoes, black and brown belts, a black beanie hat, a peaked hat, a beige hand-towel, white socks, boxer shorts and briefs.

Trevor had also packed small weights which he would Velcro around his wrists or ankles as he walked, in order to build muscles. These items were also missing.

I sent the list to Judge Marien, full of expectation. I never got a reply. I didn't even receive confirmation of what was found and what wasn't. Apart from the very first night I set foot in Saint-

Quentin in 1987, I had not seen Trevor's belongings since.

I made a new request to Judge Marien to see Trevor's things, both the belongings that had been recovered on and around his body when he was found, and in the rucksack when it was retrieved from Lac Du Der. I knew there were a lot of items missing and I had a pretty strong idea where they were. Unfortunately I couldn't get anywhere near them.

In April 1991, Judge Marien got in touch again, this time to say he was returning Trevor's watch to me by post via the Department of Foreign Affairs. It was the only piece of Trevor's belongings that I ever had returned to me. I assumed I would get a formal letter from the Department saying the watch had arrived with them. Perhaps, given the sensitive nature of the situation, someone might even come out to the house and deliver the watch to me in private. I knew that whatever happened, it would be an extremely emotional time for me and for the rest of the family. I waited for word of its arriving, but nothing happened.

Later that year, in December 1991, I received a surprise letter from Judge Marien. I had to find a translator and quick. A few days later a friend of a friend who spoke French was able to do a translation. The letter informed me of the results of Trevor's autopsy and how there was 'agreement' or similarity between soil samples from Trevor's body and a spade used by Chanel that had been recovered from his van in 1989. This was all new information to me. In his letter, the judge said that Trevor was strangled. He wrote 'there was concordance between the soil samples taken from the soil where Trevor was found and a spade belonging to Chanal. The investigators at the moment are directing suspicions towards Chanal who is homosexual and presumed the murderer of the other army boys.'

Here, finally, was confirmation that Chanal was the main suspect in my son's murder. But in the very next line, all hopes of bringing this man to trial for Trevor's murder were dashed. Judge Marien wrote, 'That being said, there is not enough evidence for charges to prove the guilt of Chanal of the murder of your son Trevor. The file is still open and the murderer unknown.' I read the note over and over again in the futile hope that I had missed the important bit that said they had found my son's killer and were bringing him to trial.

I was devastated. Even though Chanal was identified as the chief suspect, there wasn't enough evidence to bring charges against him. I didn't know much about the French legal system or the machinations of French law, but this seemed ludicrous to me. This pronouncement from Judge Marien would come back into play many years later, but in the meantime, what could I do next? It looked like I had reached the end of the road with Trevor's case.

I had to do something, anything, to keep myself busy. I decided to check all these facts for myself. I would start with the autopsy report, which I had been given when I brought Trevor's body home. Perhaps I could get a second opinion. I was beginning to question the French authorities and losing confidence that justice would ever be done for Trevor. I asked myself who would know about autopsy reports. I wanted to be clear as to what the French had done and how they had gone about it. I consulted the phone book and found the number for Garda Headquarters in the Phoenix Park. Dr Maureen Smyth was Head of Toxicology and I figured she would be the right person to give me a second opinion on the autopsy report. She was very helpful and explained what the report meant.

In 1992 I got a call from a young man in the the Department of Foreign Affairs in Dublin, 'Mrs O'Keeffe, that watch is in here,' he said casually, 'you'll need to come and collect it.' I didn't quite know what he was talking about. Then it hit me. It was Trevor's watch. This would be the only lasting piece of him I would have to keep for myself. The police had told me that it was still ticking when they found Trevor's body. For them, it had proved he hadn't been dead long when they found him, but for me, it held the last precious living moments of his young life. Caught unawares, I blurted some sort of a reply to the official on the other end of the phone and put the receiver down. I cried for a long time. Later that day, I went mournfully to the department's offices on St Stephen's Green and waited in the public lobby as a young man – I don't know if it was the same one – came out to me, handed me the watch, which I then signed for before he walked off back to his office. Maybe he thought it was my watch and that I'd lost it abroad and had simply popped in to reclaim it. I doubt he knew the significance of it for me. I breathed in deeply, not wanting to make a show of myself in such a public place. I didn't cry. I gently enfolded the watch in a handkerchief, placed it in my bag, took another deep breath and left.

For the next few years I led a double life. Day in, day out, I tortured myself with schemes and plans to nail the man who had murdered my son. When I could afford it, Noeleen and I would go to France to see if there was anything new we could find out. At the same time I also got on with running a family and my new business in Naas. I had finally hit upon the right job for me. I gave up my taxi licence to start a School of Motoring business that allowed me to pay bills at home and to the lawyers and work my own hours. It was also a sentimental reminder of the time when the kids were small and I'd teach them to drive on our holidays in Wexford. Even today I still think of my own kids when I'm teaching people to drive and I always smile when I remember Trevor raised up by his cushions in order to reach the steering wheel. I loved being my own boss and I loved working with the clients, seeing them progress from utter novices to responsible drivers. I took the business seriously, building up a good portfolio of clients and making sure I got good referrals from those who passed their tests. I was always going, going, going. I couldn't ever seem to sit still or relax.

Trevor's case was never far from my mind, whether I was working or not. Sometimes I would be in the car with a learner driver and a thought or question would come into my head and I would have to ask the client to stop the car beside a phone box, get out and call my lawyer or Foreign Affairs or Caroline or Noeleen. I couldn't possibly wait and call later. I had to make the call there and then. This was also in the days before mobile phones and I spent a fortune on phone cards – hundreds of them. I felt guilty if I let Trevor's case disappear from my mind even for a moment.

I was still writing to whomever I could think of who might help me. One young man in Foreign Affairs had been particularly helpful and had brought myself and Noeleen into his office and was most sympathetic. However, within a year or so he had moved on, and for many years afterwards I would call and get a different person to whom I would have to explain the case all over again from the beginning.

I spent a lot of time and money on translations of French documents. I came up with all sorts of ideas as to who I could call upon to do the job and I even traded free driving lessons for French translations with one lady learner who happened to be a French teacher.

We continued to wait for a meeting with Judge Marien. Meanwhile, Noeleen, thinking well ahead, came up with a novel way of how we could conduct our business despite the language problem and make sure that we would cover all our questions in our longed-for meeting. Handing me a hardback ruled notebook, she took command. 'Right,' she ordered, 'Question 1, what do we need to say here?' I offered a question. Noeleen wrote it down and then wrote an 'A' below it, allowing space for the answer. In this fashion we worked through all that we needed to ask, numbering the questions and answers as we went along. The plan was that in the meeting we'd each have a notebook with all the questions, I would ask the questions and Noeleen would take note of the answers. If I forgot a question or got waylaid by an answer, she could prompt me or ask the missed question. This meant we would never lose out on getting the answer to any one question.

Initially the questions related to how Trevor died: was he sexually assaulted, what was he killed with, what evidence did they find at the scene? As the years progressed and the case became more complicated, we needed to adopt subheadings with their own questions that related to the various aspects of the case, such as the police evidence and the judicial investigation. We used this system for all our meetings with people in authority connected with the case and, by and large, it worked pretty well. Generally, Noeleen and I weren't able to communicate with each other in those meetings, so if I forgot to ask a question, Noeleen would give me a prod with her pen and I would know that I had forgotten something. Or something might be said that sidetracked me, and Noeleen was on hand to get back to the questions we needed answered without diversion.

I called Noeleen one day, 'You'll never guess where we're going next week?'

'Where?' she asked

'Amiens,' I said, trying to sound calm.

'I don't believe you,' she laughed, 'you mean we've actually got a meeting with the judge?'

'Yes, we have,' I replied, thoroughly satisfied with myself.

By this time, we had been waiting five frustrating years to meet the investigating magistrate in Trevor's case, Judge Charles Marien. In that time I had received a lot of help from a sympathetic young woman called Elizabeth McCullough who was Second Secretary at the Irish Embassy in Paris; it was she who had helped set up this meeting and would accompany us to translate.

On Monday, 25 October 1994, just before 2pm, Noeleen and I fidgeted nervously outside Judge Marien's chambers in the impressive northeastern cathedral town of Amiens. Clutching our hardback ruled notebooks, we felt like students who were about to see the headmaster. Elizabeth McCullough joined us, so at least we could relax our worries on the language front. The door opened and Judge Marien welcomed us into his office. He was in his forties, plain-looking but polite and welcoming, initially. Noeleen and I simultaneously opened our notebooks. I cleared my throat, adjusted my glasses and started the meeting by asking about the hairs that had been found in Chanal's van and whether they could be connected to Trevor. I was nervous but determined to get some answers. Judge Marien appeared nonplussed. He said he was waiting for a report to come through and until then could say nothing about the hairs. However, he did say that they were old and had no roots in them but that the machines doing the test were foolproof. I then asked to see the underwear that I believed had also been retrieved from Chanal's van. He said that nothing in the van had an English label so therefore there could be nothing of Trevor's in the van. I asked had Trevor been sexually assaulted. 'No, no, no,' he cooed; it was because Trevor had not been assaulted in this way that he had not thought of Chanal as being the perpetrator. I was to find out much later that, in fact, Trevor's jeans had been torn and that a button was missing from his shirt when he was found, both of which pointed to the possibility of a sexual assault. How could the investigating magistrate, whose job it was to assess all the evidence passed on to him by the police, have missed these vital signs, and worse, failed to act upon them?

The judge continued by saying that Trevor had been strangled with piano wire. I found this impossible to believe. When I was young, we had used piano wire at home to slice cheese and I believed that if Trevor had been killed with piano wire, he would have had completely different injuries from the ones I'd witnessed in the photographs police had shown me. I momentarily lost my thread of questioning as I thought to myself, does this man take me for a bloody fool? Noeleen prodded me with her pen to continue.

I was not at all happy with the way Judge Marien was dealing with our questions. And worse was yet to come. In fact, the meeting descended into something of a French farce.

I asked to see Trevor's rucksack and his belongings. Judge Marien confidently informed me he didn't have the rucksack. It was in Chalons-sur-Marne, at least 80km away in another jurisdiction and to which he had no access. He said it might take one, two, or possibly more days to request the rucksack, then have it sent from his colleague, the judge in Chalons . The man was too charming to be true. I was in no mood to be fobbed off. 'Fine,' I said, I'll wait the extra days.' He seemed momentarily disarmed, then said, 'Well, it might take longer than that again.'

'Fine,' I repeated. 'Sure if it takes a week, we'll wait until we see it.'

I was determined to stay for as long as it would take for the rucksack to be sent the 80km from Chalons-sur-Marne. I couldn't believe it would take a whole week, but then everything took so long to get done, maybe it would. At this point Judge Marien's demeanour changed completely and the charming smile we'd been treated to throughout the meeting dropped from his face. He regarded me sternly. He said nothing. Then he simply got up from his chair, went over to a door, opened it, went inside and came back with a rucksack in his hand. He threw it on the ground at our feet and said, 'Is that it?'

We were dumbfounded. He had the rucksack all along? No explanation, no apology, nothing. We couldn't believe it. Right there before our very eyes he had said that the rucksack was 80 km away, when all the time it was in the next room. It took a while for this to sink in: a judge had just lied to us.

Just what sort of a situation had we got ourselves into, we asked each other as we left the judge's chambers. What exactly were we dealing with here? We had a police force that wouldn't talk to us and now we had a magistrate we couldn't trust. Who on earth was there left to help us?

CHAPTER 5

The Triangle of Death and the 'Disappeared' of Mourmelon

In 1993, while Pierre Chanal was in prison serving his ten-year sentence, I met Dominique Rizet, a journalist for the popular Paris newspaper, *France-Soir*. We met at the court where Chanal was appearing. A judge from Chalons-sur-Marne [renamed Chalons-en-Champagne in 1994], a town in the midst of the 'Triangle of Death' area, had ordered an investigation into the role of Pierre Chanal in the cases of five missing conscripts: Patrice Dubois, Serge Havet, Pascal Sergent, Patrick Denis and Patrick Gache. Now Chanal had been charged with the disappearances and was due to appear in court. Caroline had alerted us to the fact that the case was coming up. Noeleen and I made it our business to get to France to find out what was happening. We knew there was some connection with Trevor's murder, but we just didn't know how to follow it up or prove it. While we couldn't get into the court itself, we waited outside in the hope that we would pick up some information as to what was going on.

Dominique Rizet, overhearing our accents and assuming that we were connected to Trevor, came over to us and politely introduced himself. He asked if there was any way he could talk to us later in the hotel. He looked honest and unthreatening. We said yes. As a rule, Noeleen and I didn't talk to reporters because we didn't know exactly what was going on and we didn't want to prejudice Trevor's investigation in any way. Also, we didn't trust them. We trusted no one in France.

For me, not trusting reporters was a simple case of not wanting people poking about in my business. Some journalists, both at home and in France, had fabricated stories about Trevor's death, especially when I wouldn't talk to them. They would ask for five minutes of my time to talk about the case, then print only the gory details or half-truths, and sometimes no semblance of the truth at all. From an early stage I had felt it was important for me to keep control over the story. Trevor was my son, I knew him and the last thing I wanted was for someone who didn't know him, had never met him or any of our family, making up stories about him or how he died. His death was horrific enough without adding further insult to his memory. I felt that if I hadn't been able to protect him in life, then I certainly would do my damnedest to protect him in death. And that meant not talking to journalists who would twist the truth about him.

With Dominique, however, it was different. He came to our hotel and was upfront about his intentions. Without any prompting from us, he promised that he would never write anything that wasn't true. It may seem simple, but to Noeleen and I, it meant everything. Dominique seemed a nice young man. He was in his mid thirties, was clean cut, very presentable and not cocky. He was genuine and had a gentle manner, not pushy. We both liked him straight away and instinctively we felt we could trust him. We didn't quite appreciate it then, but Dominique Rizet was to have a major impact on us and our campaign. We also didn't foresee that today, thirteen years later, we would have come to regard him as a friend.

Dominique told us that he had been in communication with Pierre Chanal's sister, Simone, and that he had the whole story from her point of view, including Chanal's background and family. Through the sister, he had also met Chanal's mother. He knew that an interview with me would mean losing the trust of the Chanal family. But he was prepared to do that. We respected him for both his honesty and integrity.

The next day Dominique brought us to his newspaper office in Paris. As we followed him through bustling corridors and offices, past banks of journalists tapping away at computers, Noeleen and I hoped no one would notice that behind our confidence we felt absolutely lost; we had no idea what we were doing. We traded knowing glances; at least we felt that we were doing something.

Dominique opened a big cupboard in his office and showed us the articles he had written, mostly about Chanal, and those written after interviews with Chanal's family. He also showed us files he had on Pierre Chanal and the 'Disappeared of Mourmelon'. The cupboard was packed with files. In amongst them was a file he had marked 'Trevor O'Keeffe'. He wanted to show us that he knew the story, had been following the events most closely and was on an investigation himself to link Chanal with the 'Disappeared' and Trevor. He went into great detail. For the first time, all the threads of Trevor's case were coming together and finally making sense. Dominique revealed that, in 1988, two days after his arrest for the abduction of the young Hungarian, Pierre Chanal had also been questioned about Trevor's murder. This was shocking news to me. I knew nothing of the questioning of Chanal. I had my suspicions from newspaper articles which had linked Chanal with Trevor's murder, but this was the first time I was hearing it all in such detail and from someone I trusted.

Dominique seemed amazed at my lack of knowledge, both of French law and in particular of my rights in this serious case. He asked if I had made myself '*partie civile*' to the case, but neither myself nor Noeleen really understood what that meant. We knew nothing of French law and its processes. Antoine Comte had sought to have me informed of anything new in Trevor's case as far back as 1988. However, he had been told by the investigating magistrate that Chanal had nothing to do with Trevor's case, and I had got nowhere with the authorities myself.

Dominique explained that, in French law, if you constitute yourself a 'civil party' to a case, this gives you access to the magistrate's file, to all the evidence that has been accumulated and investigated by the police in the case. All this time when Noeleen and I had been stumbling around in the dark, we could have had access to Trevor's file. Talking to Dominique, I felt as though a light had been switched on.

Dominique phoned a lawyer whom he knew, Eric Dupond-Moretti, and asked him to meet with us with a view to taking a criminal case against Chanal. Dominique told us that Eric was one of the five top lawyers in France. Eric agreed to take on the case. We couldn't believe our luck. We really felt that things were starting to move. Dominique himself was committed to making Chanal's arrest and charge for the murder of Trevor and the other young 'Disappeared' his own campaign. At last, Noeleen and I felt we had someone to support us. And now, with Eric on our side, we felt confident of getting justice for my son.

Within a week or two of Dominique's call to Eric Dupond-Moretti, he came to visit me in Ireland. The meeting took place in Noeleen's house in Rathcoole. Eric had said he couldn't work for us if he didn't know us. He came for one day and said, tell me everything. So I did. We talked into the night and right through to the next morning when Eric had to return to France.

Eric had very little English so Dominique translated for him, even though at that time Dominique's English would not have been as good as it is today. Needless to say, my French was non-existent. It was a real struggle and very difficult at times but we all persevered, and as the night wore on, the language problem seemed to melt away. In its place came the pain of telling what I knew about Trevor's death. It was an excruciating night. I could barely talk. I had a lump in my throat that nearly choked me and yet I had to get the words out. I can't believe I actually sat in one place long enough to tell the story. Even though my son had been dead for six years, this was the first time I'd told anyone outside the family the full story, going right back to the night I got the telephone call from Tootsie.

I went through each and every detail of what had happened in Trevor's case up to that moment; how Trevor had gone to France with Christian Jaillet and then how Tootsie had got a call from him saying he couldn't find work and was coming home; how the next we heard was that a business card of Tootsie's boss was found beside a dead body. I described the wait I'd had to find out if it was Trevor who had been found, yet hoping that it wasn't him; the flight to France to identify his body, only to discover that he had been buried hours before we had arrived. Eric let out a scream of indignation when he heard this piece of information; he couldn't believe the insensitivity of the police. After all, they must have known I was coming to identify the body because they had booked me into a hotel. I told Eric how I had never spoken with the Jaillet family and that they had not contacted me since Trevor's death.

Eric was clear in his advice. If we had any hope of bringing Chanal to trial for Trevor's murder, I could not prejudice a future case in any way. I was not allowed to accuse Chanal of anything in public. At the time, I didn't think this was a difficult request. I believed we would be going to trial soon enough. I had no idea that it would be another decade before a trial would take place and that, during the bulk of that time, Chanal, who was currently in prison for a sickening crime meted out on a defenceless young man, would be allowed back into society and be free as a bird.

At the end of the night, Eric told me he would do everything he could to pursue the case. Although exhausted, I was hopeful for the first time in all the years since Trevor was murdered.

When Eric returned to Paris the next day, the first thing he did was to exert whatever pressure he could to have Chanal charged in relation to Trevor's murder. Eric encouraged me to do interviews in the media as a way of highlighting the case and the problems we'd had until then. Dominique interviewed me for *France-Soir* where I detailed the delays, lack of information and faceless bureaucracy I had endured for the last six years in trying to get my son's case heard.

A few weeks later, Noeleen and I went back to France. Dominique had been busy and had set up a meeting with one of the founders of the 'Disappeared of Mourmelon' organisation, Jean

Du Pont. It struck me as ludicrous that we were now going to meet a founder of an organisation that the police had told us didn't exist! Jean Du Pont was a retired small farmer who had made the linking of Chanal to the 'Disappeared of Mourmelon' his life's work. He was a little man but he walked with great purpose. We used to call him 'The Judge' because he was so commanding. Myself, Noeleen and Caroline met Dominique and Jean off a train in Chantilly in Northern France and went to a bar there where Jean told us everything he knew. He didn't have a word of English so Dominique and Caroline had to do all the translating for us. What he told us was astonishing.

We spent a whole day with him and time flew by as he talked. He had scrutinised every detail of Chanal's testimony during the court case in relation to the abduction of Palazs Falvay. He then spent his own money buying a van just like Chanal's distinctive green Volkswagen, mapped out the routes that Chanal claimed he had taken and set about disproving them, one by one. He travelled miles along the autoroutes and could see when Chanal would have needed to stop for refuelling. In Trevor's case, he claimed that Chanal was on the road from which Trevor disappeared. He claimed that Chanal would have stopped six times for petrol. This studious collection of information was an obsession with him but it was all very encouraging to me. He could tell us every move Chanal had made, what garage he had stopped at on any one of his travels, and how long it took for him to get from one place to another. One thing was for sure, Jean was convinced that Chanal was not only the man who murdered Trevor but had also murdered many other young men.

A day later, Dominique took us to meet Madame Havet, whose

name had been given to us by Caroline in connection with 'The Disappeared of Mourmelon', but who we hadn't known how to contact. She too had been involved in setting up the organisation. Unlike Jean Du Pont, however, she had a more visceral reason for being involved: her son, Serge was one of 'The Disappeared'.

We drove for miles down twisted narrow roads to get to Madame Havet's house near Reims, about an hour outside Paris. It was a good job Dominique knew where he was going because I certainly didn't. The pretty countryside slid by in a blur. We arrived at a small house with a lovely garden where the family grew their own vegetables. Madame Havet showed us into her sitting room that she had turned into a shrine to her son, with photographs of him, surrounded by many holy pictures, covering the wall. She was glamorous, blonde-haired and had a very commanding presence. She never stopped talking. It seemed that she could not get the words out quick enough. I don't know how Dominique kept up with her! In the end he translated what he felt was appropriate to us.

Madame Havet gave us all the details of her son's disappearance, or as much detail as she knew at the time. Serge, a good-looking boy with wavy dark hair, was only twenty-one years old and a conscript with the 3rd artillery regiment. He disappeared after getting leave to visit his family on 20 February, 1981. His car had broken down and he was thumbing a lift back to the barracks. He was never seen again and his body had not been recovered. 'At least,' Madame Havet said to me, 'you have your son; his body was found. We had no news, not one word and no body.' I needed no translation for the bitter regret I detected in her voice. I felt real sorrow for her.

In the midst of all the talking, she told us something about the way the investigation was handled that made me uneasy. Apparently, Jean-Marie Tarbes, the policeman who was handling her son's case, had become very involved in all the 'Disappeared' cases and showed real determination in finding the killer. He was amassing lots of evidence and had befriended her and some of the other parents. However, he was unexpectedly moved from her town before he could conclude his enquiries. We wondered if this had been a deliberate move by the authorities, and if so, why?

Madame Havet told us about the other boys. According to her, there were up to sixteen young men whose deaths were unaccounted for during an eight-year period in the 1980s, but only seven families had cases currently with investigating magistrates. Noeleen and I looked at each other. If all these young men, including Trevor, had been murdered by the same person, we were not only dealing with a dangerous serial killer but someone who had successfully eluded the police for over a decade. How on earth had this person got away with so much for so long? Had the army sergeant, Pierre Chanal, committed all these murders? And if so, how had he not been caught before now?

Patrice Dubois of the 4th tank regiment at Mourmelon disappeared on 4 January 1980. Desertion proceedings were begun. Serge Havet disappeared on 20 February 1981. Manuel Carvalho of the 4th dragoon regiment at Mourmelon went on a week's leave and disappeared on 7 August 1981. Pascal Sargent of the 503rd tank regiment at Mourmelon did not return from leave on 20 August 1981. As with most of the young men who disappeared, there was little urgency to do anything about their disappearances since the authorities believed they had deserted from their

National Service, as over 6,000 did every year.

In some cases, parents who had not heard from their sons in weeks and sometimes a month would call the barracks, only to be told their son was not available to take the call. They only found out afterwards that their sons had been missing all along. The army has, to my knowledge never discussed their reasoning with the families in public, even to this day.

Then, on 31 October 1982, the body of Olivier Donner of the 503rd tank regiment at Mourmelon was found hidden under brushwood near Mailly-Le-Camp. He had been in the same regiment as Patrice Dubois and Manuel Carvalho. He had phoned his sister to tell her he was on his way to his home town of Troyes. Friends had left him to the RN77 main road from where he would hitchhike. That was on 30 September. No one had seen him for a month. His distraught parents insisted on an investigation – this was certainly not a desertion situation. His body was found with no identification, near a main road, in an accessible place, but hidden under branches. There were no houses nearby. Unfortunately, the body was so decomposed that it yielded few clues as to how he had been killed.

At Donner's parents' insistence, a judicial investigation began in Troyes and the existence of a serial killer in the area began to be suspected. However, on 2 August 1984, and with no more disappearances recorded since the finding of Olivier Donner, the files on Dubois, Havet, Sargent, Carvalho and Donner were closed. The police investigation had ground to a halt for lack of evidence. In particular, the fact that the bodies of the other four had not been found meant that the police and investigating magistrates had virtually nothing to go on. I understood that while there was enough evidence to implicate Chanal and have him interrogated, there was not enough to complete the file for forwarding to the State Prosecutor. Judicial authorities in various districts took the line for a long time that although Chanal was the likely murderer, it could have been others.

Years later I discovered that Pierre Chanal had been posted to Beirut from January to May 1985, and this was used as evidence against him, since there were no disappearances during that time. He was quick to counter the argument, saying that from August 1984 to January 1985, when he *was* around, there were no disappearances either.

On 23 August 1985, Patrice Denis disappeared on his way to the Mourmelon camp. The television technician, a civilian, was going to the camp to see the launch of experimental rockets. He was hitchhiking on the RN77 around 17.30 but never arrived at the camp. In the case of the other 'Disappeared', who were conscripts, there was a general belief that they had deserted. However, no such excuse was available for the disappearance of Denis, a civilian, and a police investigation began, spearheaded by policeman Jean-Marie Tarbes under the direction of a Captain Vaillant, which led to a judicial enquiry into the 'abduction' of Patrice Denis in Chalons-en-Champagne.

Meanwhile, Patrick Gache of the 4th dragoon regiment at Mourmelon left the camp on 30 April 1987 and failed to return. He had left the army base around 6pm to walk to the local railway station, two miles away, from where he would catch a train home for four days' leave over the May holiday. He did not arrive at the station and was never seen again. This disappearance happened only months before Trevor was murdered. The 2,700 inhabitants of Mourmelon and all the men at the army base were interviewed. In fact, all persons over the age of fifteen were questioned but no one was charged. There were rumours circulating at the time about the involvement of religious sects and homosexual circles. Any hitchhikers in the area who had been the object of threats or unusual behaviour were also questioned. Searches for the bodies of other 'Disappeared' were carried out then but yielded no results or clues. The police had previously carried out surveillance on the routes near the camps in August 1986 and repeated the process from July to September 1987 at certain times of the day. However, the surveillance revealed nothing unusual. Pierre Chanal was also questioned in 1986, and, whether coincidental or not, was transferred to Fontainebleau Barracks around the same time.

The similarities between the 'Disappeared of Mourmelon' and Trevor's murder were startling: young men between eighteen and twenty-one, hitchhiking, vanishing within a 15km zone around Reims-Mailly. And, inevitably, the finger of suspicion pointed to Mourmelon military camp, with which most of the 'Disappeared' were associated, and where Pierre Chanal had been based in the years of the disappearances.

However, the absence of bodies, except for that of Olivier Donner, meant that that the French judges could not consider a prosecution, despite the best efforts of the missing boys' parents. And even in the Donner case, the body was so decomposed when it was found that the autopsy proved inconclusive. That meant that the only body which had been found and could be tied to Chanal was Trevor's. Trevor would, therefore, be a key part of one of the biggest murder mysteries in France.

In 1994, I at last gained access to Chanal's file. From it I learned that statements had been taken from a number of young recruits in 1988 in the Mourmelon camp. A pattern was emerging in relation to Chanal, dating as far back as 1979, as to how he conducted himself with those who served under him.

A recruit who was drafted into the 4th regiment in Mourmelon in 1979 said that his first three weeks were OK, but in January 1980, Chanal changed suddenly and was violent, raining insults and blows on the recruits for no apparent reason. He would delay conscripts from going on leave,' losing' their leave forms and then suddenly finding them again, but only when the buses had left the barracks and they would be forced to hitchhike. While he did not remember any specific incidents of a 'homosexual nature', this young recruit did note that Chanal always managed to do a tour of inspection at 2pm when the lads were in the showers. Still more worryingly, he noted that when a recruit had been sodomised by others, some had intervened to stop it and a fight had broken out. Those responsible for the sodomy were put in the cells. Everyone except Chanal supported those who had intervened; Chanal said that they shouldn't have and that it 'was nothing dramatic'.

Another recruit, drafted in 1981, said that Chanal was a hard man with a sadistic tendency and liked to see boys suffer in manoeuvres. Again he stated that Chanal would refuse to sign leave orders, for reasons unknown.

One young lad who had been drafted in June 1982 said that Chanal was an authoritarian figure. When he was in charge of giving permission to go on leave, he 'used to check our bags, would send people back to the dormitories if the bags weren't in order; he could not prevent people leaving but could delay it.'

Some months after this recruit was drafted, a soldier's body was found near the main road. He recognised the body from a photo. It was Olivier Donner. There was an inquiry in the regiment. Chanal addressed all the recruits, advising them against hitchhiking and above all to take care who they got into a car with.

Another young recruit, drafted in April 1982, had known the missing conscript, Olivier Donner, and used to give him a lift when he could. When Donner disappeared, Chanal called his friend into his office to ask him what he knew. It was as if Chanal was carrying out his own personal inquiry. He accused the recruit of having taken Donner into the countryside and left him there 'after some sort of problem'. The ad hoc interrogation lasted an hour, and throughout that period Chanal gave the impression that the whole squad belonged to him and that he was its master in every way.

The recruit also said that Chanal would get a kick out of keeping conscripts back so that they would miss their train when they were going on leave. He would inspect their rooms, say they weren't clean enough and order a re-inspection at the time the buses left for the station. He then took his time about it. A sergeant once told Chanal that this wasn't allowed, but Chanal's reply was that he didn't give a damn about it and that he was in charge. He was violent, kicking and punching conscripts when they didn't do as they were told. Even his superiors were afraid of him. On one occasion he even slammed a superior against a wall, mistaking him for a conscript.

One of the recruits noted that while they never saw Chanal pick up anyone, he would routinely drive slowly on the Chalons to Mourmelon road between 6pm and 7pm when the recruits would be going off on leave.

In all, Chanal's reputation in the army barracks was of a highly skilled, tough, sadistic and often violent soldier who thought he was untouchable. It certainly seemed possible that he had both the qualities and experience needed to be capable of killing and of disposing of bodies in such a way that they might never be found. However, we still couldn't understand how so many young men could disappear and the investigation not find a culprit. There seemed to have been a lot of police activity surrounding these cases from the early 1980s and yet no one had been charged and brought to court.

We had arranged another meeting with Judge Marien and, armed with our notebooks, Noeleen and I went to see him. Again, Elizabeth McCullough joined us to translate. I opened my book and started with the same question I had been asking for some time, both orally and by letter: 'Is there any chance I could go into Chanal's quarters in his barracks and see if there was anything of Trevor's that might be there?' 'I'm afraid that's not possible,' replied the judge. He was stoney-faced but polite. The meeting came to an end. I was no further on. No matter what I asked, I felt I was getting nowhere. I looked at Noeleen. I knew what she was thinking because it was the same thought I had: Chanal is being protected.

The next morning I talked it over with Noeleen. 'I'll accept the decision of the court so long as Chanal is tried,' I said. I was convinced that if we got him into court he would be found guilty. Noeleen and I both were. I said to Noeleen, 'I'll let the court deal with him, but if they let him out, I will shoot him myself.' She knew I wasn't joking.

A week later, Eric called with the good news: Chanal was being charged with Trevor's murder. Since he had told me to raise the profile of the case through more media interviews, I had, reluctantly, taken part in news programmes for French television and gave a lot of interviews in the print media. I had gone from not telling anyone of what happened to Trevor to now telling anyone who would listen, in the hope that it would have some affect on the case. I was amazed that not only had Eric worked a minor miracle but that the media could actually make a difference. It changed my whole perspective. However, this good news was not to last.

When it came to it, Chanal was charged only with 'voluntary homicide', a lesser charge that, in Eric's opinion was absolutely stupefying. Judge Marien, along with his chief prosecutor, Patrick Quincy at Saint-Quentin, had announced that the charge would give Chanal the chance to 'defend himself against public accusations'. He told the press that Chanal would be under investigation but would have access to the file against him. Following Judge Marien's decision, Eric got in touch with me to explain the situation. 'It's unbelievable,' he raged, and we sent a letter to the judge in November 1994. Eric pointed out that this type of charge was not usually made just so the accused could defend himself and that the judge's actions were changing the spirit of the law as regards placing persons under investigation. Eric gave interviews to the press and didn't hold back with his opinions on the charge against Chanal.

In the meantime, I was only interested in getting Chanal into a courtroom. I phoned Eric and said, 'Look, we've come this far, we'll keep going. I know Chanal will have to explain himself in court, and for me, that would be the most important thing. I want to know what he did to my son and I don't care how we get there.'

I suddenly felt confident and bold, capable of anything. I could see the way ahead and it was looking better than it had done for a long time.

We arranged to meet Eric in his office in Lille, 80km outside Paris. As per usual, Noeleen booked the flights. Caroline would not be picking us up. We were on our own this time, and more importantly, it was my job to get us to our destination. Now, while I might be an ace driver and navigator at home, when it came to getting around in a foreign country, in a different language and on the wrong side of the road, I was a different person altogether. And it didn't help that I had to luck out in front of my very organised big sister. We made our way from the airport to Paris and the Gare Du Nord train station, from where we boarded the train to Lille. So far, so good. It took most of the day but Noeleen had insisted we give ourselves loads of time to get there. As we stepped off the train, I reached into my bag to get Eric's address and telephone number. I pulled out some paper that I thought was the address but which turned out to be just a bill. I was starting to panic but wouldn't dare show it.

'Oh, here it is, here it is,' I said brightly, pulling out other bits of paper, none of which looked familiar. Without looking up, I could sense Noeleen rolling her eyes at me. 'Oh, I think I have it here, I have it here,' I said, upending the entire contents of my bag onto a nearby bench. Noeleen was not amused. 'We've come all this way and you've no address?' she said sternly.

I thought she was going to kill me so I didn't look at her. I looked for a phone box instead. I had to call Bill back home and, thank God, he was in. 'Could you look out Eric's address for me?' I asked, trying to sound nonchalant.

'You've gone all that way and you've no address?' he asked.

'Yeah, yeah, who would have believed it, eh?' I laughed lightly, giving the thumbs-up to Noeleen outside the phone box. 'I'll call you back in a few minutes, Bill, OK?' I waited ten minutes, rang back and got the address and phone number. 'I have it now, Noeleen, not too much of a setback, really.' She didn't respond and we went off to find a taxi to take us to Eric's office.

We got into the back seat of the taxi, having told the driver where we needed to go. I knew Noeleen was back to her normal self when I saw the map coming out of her bag. 'Yes, I think he's going the right way, Eroline,' she said authoritatively. 'Oh yes,' I replied, 'sure I remember this street all right myself.'

Noeleen had come up with this plan involving a map and us pretending we knew where we were going so as to deter any rip-off taxi drivers who might want to take a couple of middle-aged foreign ladies on an unplanned sightseeing tour. We had been stung a few times before, and, on one occasion, had we known it, we could have seen our destination from the train station we stepped out of. Unfortunately, we only realised our mistake after we'd paid for a particularly circuitous taxi journey.

Finally we got to Eric's office in one piece and without being ripped off. We were in good spirits and would have liked to chat. However, our meeting was quick and to the point.

Within three weeks of my meeting with Eric, I would be face to face with the man who murdered my son.

CHAPTER 6

Assembling the Jigsaw

Eric arranged for a summary of the investigation file and related documents on Trevor to be sent to me, and for the first time in six years I was able to read information that was vital to understanding how my son had died, including the autopsy report and what the investigators found around Trevor's burial place, amongst other details. But, of course, in order to read the documentation I had to find a translator. I gave an interview to Gay Byrne on RTÉ radio, telling him of Trevor's death and the case so far. Afterwards I was surprised to receive a number of letters and phone calls of support, but one in particular stood out. It was from Éamon Ó Ciosáin, a French language lecturer from Maynooth University. He offered to translate any official documentation related to Trevor's case.

I met with Éamon and took to the young lecturer immediately – he was sympathetic but businesslike and I liked his detached yet friendly demeanour. I took the decision to entrust all my documents to him and from then on would regularly drive over to the university to drop off paperwork. Not only did he turn out to be a great help in translating documents, but he was also able to explain some of the more intricate aspects of French law to me in plain language. He even suggested questions that he felt I should be asking of the authorities. Sometimes I felt he knew Trevor's case better than I did!

Now, for the first time, I could try to piece together a more accurate picture of what had happened to Trevor than I had ever received from the police, the investigating magistrate or the newspapers. Yet the real jigsaw of what had happened would take even more years to assemble, and would come from a great many different sources. Slowly I built a picture of my son's last days.

When Trevor announced his plans to go to France with Christian Jaillet, in August 1987, James, my eldest son, said he would go too, but in the end he decided not to. Another friend of theirs also said he would think about going, but by the time he had made up his mind to go, the two lads had gone. Their destination was Christian's home place, a small town at the foot of the French Alps, called Poligny. The town itself was very pretty, with only around 5000 people and set into the foothills of the Alps. All around were vineyards and green fields. It wasn't a major tourist town but had a sizeable student population.

It took Trevor and Christian only a few days to get down through France to Poligny. I have never found out how they got there, whether by train or bus, but I reckon they probably got lifts.

When they got to Poligny, Christian's mother invited Trevor to stay with them. He looked for work but couldn't find any and after three days he decided to come home.

Neither Christian nor his family ever contacted me in the years since Trevor's death, and in the end it was me who went looking for them. In 1998, a young producer from RTÉ, Philip McGovern, approached me. He wanted to make a television documentary about Trevor. He had a good way with him and seemed genuinely interested in the details of Trevor's murder and the problems we'd had along the way with the investigation. Philip's idea was for me to go back and track Trevor's journey from Poligny to where his body, and later, his rucksack, were found and to bring it all up to date with the investigation so far.

Philip and his researcher, Brenda Moran, found out where Christian lived and got an address for him. We sent a letter telling him we would be in Poligny as part of the programme and wanted to meet him. We went to his address but he wasn't there. We also had the address of his parents, so we went there. His sister, Elizabeth, was at home and told us that Christian had, quite unusually, announced that he was going away and had just gone off, as if out of the blue. It was a most untypical thing for him to do. Now that she saw us on her doorstep, she knew why he had behaved so strangely. Christian did not want to meet us. He obviously couldn't cope with seeing us. Philip then set up a meeting between Christian's mother and myself. This was my first and only meeting with Christian's family. It was eleven years after Trevor's murder but I was desperate to hear what Trevor had said to her, how he was when he left her family, what mood he was in, was he happy and contented, was he agitated and still angry, what his last words to her might have been?

The meeting was not what I expected and I was disappointed. I wanted to hear replies to questions that were impossible for a mere stranger to answer. How on earth could I expect this French lady who barely knew my son to offer me insights into his mind? She had only met him for a few days and because of the language barrier would have hardly communicated with him. I was unexpectedly reminded of how, to them, Trevor's trip had been little more than another student coming to the town to look for work, a friend of their son's who had simply come to stay. Christian and his family could never for one moment have thought that it would end in the terrible way it did. No one did. I had to accept that the meeting would not give me any comfort but might offer some physical clues as to Trevor's last movements.

Christian's mother told me she thought Trevor had been a nice young fellow who they had welcomed into their house. She told me how upset and shocked she and her family had been when the police came to tell them about Trevor. Christian especially had been most disturbed about what happened and hence his reluctance to talk to us.

Trevor settled in with Christian's family in Poligny, but after three days of not finding work in any of the nearby vineyards or fruit fields, he announced to the family that he was returning to Ireland. I already knew from Tootsie that he had called her to say he couldn't find work and that he felt Christian's family were not well off and he didn't want to impose on them any longer. He told her not to tell me he was on his way so that it would be a surprise for me when he turned up.

With Christian's help, Trevor planned his route home carefully, writing down the names of the towns he needed to travel through on his way north to Calais: Dijon, Troyes, Chalons-sur-Marne, Reims, Saint-Quentin, then onto Calais, and from there home to Ireland. It was a distance of some 400km from Poligny to Calais but he was confident of making it in a few days. He planned to get across the Channel by ferry, taking a lift in a lorry. Although he appeared very prepared for the trip, when his rucksack was found later, there were tent pegs missing which he had left at Christian's house, so he would have had difficulty in pitching his tent.

On Monday morning, 3 August, Trevor was taken to the main motorway route north to Paris. I'm sure he would have wanted to get going early to make the most of the day. It would have been a half hour journey from the Jaillet's home in Poligny to the motorway.

When Christian Jaillet was interviewed by the police some weeks after Trevor's body was found, he made a statement that it was he who had left Trevor to the motorway so he could thumb a lift. Although the police had taken Christian in for questioning, he was quickly released and eliminated from their enquiries.

Now, as Madame Jaillet and I talked, I was most surprised to hear her say that it was actually she who had left Trevor to the motorway. She had driven him there and had offered him money to get the train back up to Calais. She had thought it might be more comfortable for him to catch the train rather than spend days on the road hitching. I was touched that she had behaved as I would have, as I would hope any mother would in similar circumstances. However I was puzzled as to why Christian and his mother had been confused as to who drove Trevor to the motorway, offering two contradictory stories. It didn't add up. Rather than feeling enlightened by the meeting with Madame Jaillet, I came away with more questions than answers. I had no doubt the family had been deeply shocked and traumatised to hear about Trevor's death and the way he died and perhaps that explains the difference in stories. However, it was one mystery that was never cleared up. I couldn't help feeling that the facts would become clearer had I spoken to Christian himself. And I would have liked to talk to Christian as one of the last friendly faces Trevor would have seen.

Trevor had refused the offer of a train fare to Calais, saying he was happy to hitchhike. I remembered then that in fact Trevor already had money – the £30 Tootsie had given him when he left England. She told him it was contingency money, to be used in an emergency if he needed to get home quickly. Trevor never used the money; the £30 was still on his body when it was found.

From the moment Trevor stepped out of the Jaillet's car onto the motorway, it was as if he disappeared into thin air. No one ever came forward to say they had given him a lift or even spotted him on the side of the road. Just how far Trevor got before he was murdered, I'll never know, but his body was found five days later, 8 August 1987 in Alaincourt, near Saint-Quentin.

The autopsy report and subsequent investigations gave further clues as to what might have happened to Trevor after this point. The autopsy revealed, amongst other things, that Trevor had eaten before he died. He'd had a burger and chips. I wondered then, where had he eaten, and when? Did he eat in someone's company, was that someone the person who murdered him? Was it Pierre Chanal?

While Captain Skoczylas had given me some details as to how Trevor was found when I identified his body in 1987, it was a statement made by a police officer, Mr Villete, that provided me with a fuller explanation as to when the body was found and how, and what had happened to Trevor. The statement was made on 14 August 1987, following the launch of a murder investigation. I received the statement from Eric in 1994 and had it translated by Éamon:

On 8th August 1987 at 8.30pm, Monsieur Michel Lente alerted the Gendarmerie of Moy de L'Aisne to the fact that he had just discovered a body in a wooded area owned by him, at a place known as

'La Sablonnière' which is in the commune of Alaincourt. The corpse was found in said wood, situated at the side of a track, called 'La Sablonnière', about 5.5 metres from the track. The corpse was face-downwards and the face was covered in blood. It was covered with 20cms of soft clay.

No other evidence could be found at the site, except for nettles which had been crushed at the edge of the wood.

According to M. Lente, the body could only have been put there between Monday 3rd or Tuesday 4th August 1987 and Saturday 8th August before 8.30pm (the time at which he discovered the body).

The corpse was of a man in his twenties, of medium build, with brown hair. It was clothed in a blue shirt with a 'Primark' label and a black pair of jeans with a 'Lee' label, size 28-34, and a light blue underpants with an 'Ecor' label, 2 blue suede shoes made by 'Men Top', size 41 (the shoe on the right foot had been removed and placed on the body on top of the right hip), black socks. A rectangular shaped 'Citizen' watch was also found on the body and a hand-kerchief with a logo of Alibaba on his flying carpet surrounded by oriental looking buildings was found in the right hand trouser pocket.

Having access to the investigating file did not answer all my questions. In fact, the file threw up a whole barrage of inadequacies in the way the investigation was conducted and had been conducted from day one. On one of my visits to Michel Lente, in 1994, I discovered that, in fact, the police only secured the site where Trevor was found on Monday, two full days after Michel found the body and alerted the police. This meant that the scene had not been preserved for two days, a serious omission in forensic terms.

It would have been immediately obvious to the police who uncovered Trevor that the deep wound around his swollen neck meant he had been strangled. In 1996, on the orders of a new investigating magistrate, Judge Chapart, a second opinion was sought on the original autopsy findings. The pathologist, Professor Lecomte, stated that in the cases of strangulation, investigations of possible sexual assault are always to be done and that a strict procedure should be followed in this respect. However, this had not been done in Trevor's original autopsy in 1987.

Trevor's jeans had been torn below the flies and all the buttons were missing on his shirt. This would normally have alerted trained police to the possibility of a sex crime, but it seems to have been overlooked in Trevor's case, or deemed not important. In any event, it was not followed up until Eric made these important discoveries when scrutinising the photographs taken of Trevor's body as it was being uncovered in 1987. These were the same photos I had seen on my first night in Saint-Quentin, but I couldn't be certain if I had noticed the missing buttons or simply blocked the thought from my mind.

Police also found a handkerchief beside Trevor's body with the initials CHPM on it. At the time they discounted the hankerchief as evidence on the basis that the laundry label at a nearby institution bore the same initials. However CHPM also stood for Chanal, Pierre Marcel, the paratrooper's full name. There was much speculation about this among journalists and Eric believed that this piece of evidence was significant and should have been followed up. There were stains found on the handkerchief which were identified only as 'brown stains' and again discounted as having anything to do with Chanal. Even when DNA testing was brought into the case under a new investigating magistrate in 1996, these brown stains were never investigated. Examination of the scene where the body was found was limited to a search for objects only in the immediate vicinity.

According to the file, an autopsy of the body was ordered on 11 August 1987, carried out on 12 August and was delivered to the State Prosecutor on 17 August by Doctors Bernard Cathelain and Philippe Kuhn at the Saint-Quentin hospital morgue. Soil and other samples, including samples taken from under Trevor's nails and from his clothes and shoes, were sent for analysis to the Lille police laboratory. So while Trevor lay in the morgue and his body was subject to the doctors' examination, I was hundreds of miles away in Naas receiving the phone call from Tootsie that she thought Trevor might be dead. Yet it would be days before we knew where he was.

The autopsy indicated death by strangulation, using a strap or cord, taking place most likely on 3rd or 4th August. It mentioned a strangulation wound of 8mm wide. Trevor had been strangled from behind by a rope passed twice around his neck. A corresponding rope was found in Pierre Chanal's van only a year after Trevor's murder. Other strap marks found on Trevor's neck were never investigated. The second opinion, given by Professor Lecomte in his 1996 report, concluded that the original autopsy was incomplete in the context of an investigation of death by strangulation, and that a fuller post-mortem and analysis of samples from the body could have been feasible given that the death was recent.

Both reports revealed that Trevor was a strong young man, which came as no surprise to me, since I believed that, had he needed to, he would have fought hard against his attacker, particularly because of his karate training. The autopsy report noted a ring mark on the middle finger of Trevor's left hand. This came, I knew, from the silver Claddagh ring he wore on that finger. It was never recovered.

What was recovered was Trevor's rucksack, found in December 1987, four months after Trevor was murdered, by Joëlle Charuel and her husband. Trevor's rucksack, with clothes, identification papers and an itinerary of his journey home was found over 200km to the south, in Lac Du Der. The Charuels alerted the police who told them to keep it in their garage. And there it remained until Joëlle contacted me. I got in touch with police in Naas who alerted police in France who dispatched a large squad of gendarmes to the Charvel's home to retrieve the rucksack. However the contents were never subject to any analysis.

The forensic report on the soil and other samples sent to the Lille police laboratory appeared in June 1988, ten months after receipt of the samples. However, it was not signed and it was not clear whether one, two or three persons mentioned in the report had actually carried it out. In 1996, Judge Chapart ordered a new report on this forensic examination that came back with some damning conclusions: the samples taken from under Trevor's nails were observed, very briefly, but not analysed. There was considerable vagueness in the terminology used to describe soil and blood, and the usual conventions used for forensic descriptions of soil types and grains were not used. No haematologist appeared to have been involved in the blood tests. Also, several potential pieces of evidence had been left unanalysed.

Police bungling of the investigation would only be part of the farce that constituted the examination of my son's murder.

Pierre Chanal would probably never have been suspected nor brought to court for any murders had it not been for the chance discovery in 1988 of the terrified and brutalised young Hungarian hitchhiker, Palazs Falvay in the back of Chanal's van.

The unmasking of Chanal with the arrest and charge of abduction and rape of Palazs Falvay, was to have a crucial bearing on the evidence available not only to Trevor's case but to all the families of the Disappeared. Palazs Falvay's testimony, along with the examination of Chanal's van, yielded a wealth of new clues. It was also a source of new heartbreak as I struggled with the gruesome detail of Palazs' torture and hoped against hope that Trevor had not been subjected to the same.

In 1988, as I wept in a Naas graveyard on the first anniversary of Trevor's death, Pierre Chanal was already being questioned by detectives from Amiens and Saint-Quentin, not only about Trevor's murder but about the fate of the 'Disappeared of Mourmelon'. Within days, police had discovered that the Palazs Falvay crime was not an isolated incident. In follow-up searches, they discovered a raft of bizarre pieces of evidence that could link Chanal to the disappearance of others. He had a collection of home-made pornographic videos that showed young men being abused. He had video camera equipment as well as sound recording equipment. He had a vibrator, khaki straps from a gas mask and a section of chain that Chanal claimed he was going to use for a door in Mourmelon base. He had thirty-two pairs of underpants of different sizes, shapes and colours, only a fraction of which would have fitted him. One pair, a Marks and Spencer pair, matched exactly a pair belonging to Trevor. He had dumbbells for weight-training, at least one with reddish marks on it that Chanal could not explain.

He also had a squeezable rubber ball used for wrist exercises. This matched one that Trevor had with him that summer and which was never recovered.

Hundreds of hair fragments were found in the van on and around a foam mattress that Chanal kept on the floor of the van. Over a hundred hairs were identified, though years later this number increased, first to 400, then, by the late 1990s when another judge took over, to an incredible 600 hairs available for testing. The testing of the hairs would become one of the most crucial elements, not only in the case of Trevor's murder, but also the disappearance of the other young men.

A spade was found with soil on it which was very different from that found on the wheels of the vehicle. Could it have been used for the burial of victims? Could it have been used to bury Trevor?

Forensic tests were carried out on the contents of the van and revealed that at least six other people had been in the van, besides Chanal himself. This was an astounding discovery; not only were the authorities dealing with a suspected abductor and rapist, but, potentially, they were dealing with a multi-murderer and one of the most dangerous serial killers France had ever known.

A well-known specialist in soil sample technology, whom the police and magistrates had used often in their work, was brought in to make the analysis of the soil found on the spade. Doctor Loïc Le Ribault had appeared in numerous articles in publications all over France. Throughout the 1980s he had built up one of France's leading forensic laboratories based on his own pioneering technique, called exoscopy. This involved the analysis of grains of quartz or sand using electron microscopy. Each grain has its own unique characteristics and Le Ribault could identify to within metres where in the world a particular grain of quartz came from.

Le Ribault went to work on soil samples taken from Chanal's spade and the site where Trevor was buried. His findings showed that both samples displayed the presence of non-natural particles of calcium sulphate. Le Ribault concluded that the soil found on Chanal's spade matched perfectly with that of the soil taken from where Trevor was buried.

However, when presented with this seemingly cast iron evidence from a distinguished and proven specialist, who had been used by the police on many previous occasions, Judge Marien decided the evidence was inconclusive. Throughout the following decade we would be doomed to arguing for the soil samples to be re-analysed. At various times the samples were said to be lost, then not sufficient for analysis. Not until a new judge took over the case in 1996 were the soil samples 'found' and re-analysed. They were indeed proven to be the same. Loïc Le Ribault had been right after all.

However it was too late for Le Ribault, as his work with the authorities stopped and eventually he was forced to close and sell up his laboratory. He cited political interference, saying his tests had exposed police incompetence and that he was being punished for it. He disappeared from public view. I met him, along with Noeleen, in one of the strangest episodes of the whole case, but not until 1998.

A statement from the investigating file on Trevor's case revealed that Pierre Chanal had been questioned about his whereabouts around the time of Trevor's death. Detectives from Amiens, under mandate from the investigating magistrate at Saint-Quentin, arrived to question him from 9.30pm on 10 August 1988 to 2am on 11 August. The Amiens police also carried out a search of his van.

In the first interview on 10 August 1988, Chanal was asked:

'What did you do in August 1987?'

'I had leave from the 1st to the 31st. On the 25th July, I was at an air meeting in Vendeuvre. I did a parachute jump with my club. To travel to Vendeuvre, I was transported in a plane which took off from Mourmelon before 9pm and I jumped above Troyes 40 minutes later. From the 27th of July to the 31st July 1987, I worked as usual in Fontainebleau.'

'When did you, in fact, go away on leave in August 1987?'

'I can't say precisely if I left Fontainebleau on the evening of the 31st or the following morning. I reached Mourmelon like every weekend on the Saturday morning (1st August) probably around 8 or 8.30am. I took part in jumps and training sessions until Sunday evening. I slept in the van as I usually do there, in the para-club car park. On Monday 3rd August 1987, I left Mourmelon around 9.15am to go to Verdun [a World War One battlefield site about 90km north of Mourmelon]. I went through Ste-Menehould to go to Verdun, I didn't take the motorway. I reached Verdun towards midday, and stayed there until Thursday the 6th August, including all day Thursday. I visited the battlefields and the monuments in the area and on the morning of the 7th August 1987 I drove off towards Lac Du Der. I parked in a carpark on the southwest bank of the lake for one day only (7/8/87).

'I spent the day reading a book about Verdun. It must have been 7pm or 7.30pm when I left the lake to return to Mourmelon for the parachute jumps the next day. I took the road through Vitry-le-Francois and Chalons and arrived at Mourmelon in the early evening. I spent the night of the 7th to 8th of August in the carpark of the Mourmelon parachute club as usual.'

Chanal was asked if he had picked up any hitchhikers on the way or from Verdun. He replied, 'I'm categorical about that, I picked up nobody.'

Why did he keep khaki straps in his van?

'They are gas-mask straps which I recover when the bags are scrapped because they are stored away without the straps. I use them to tie packages in my camping-van.'

Chanal was also asked if he had been on a commando course.

'Between 1967 and 1974, I went on four commando training courses in France and Germany.'

In answer to a question about bringing down an opponent, he detailed that one way was to use piano wire:

'You attack the guard from behind, you pass the string around his neck and cross it behind the nape of the neck, which has the effect of cutting through the windpipe artery, or the carotid artery. At each end of the piano string there are handles which make it possible to get a firm hold.' He added that, in peacetime, a nylon cord or hemp rope could be used, and had been, for learning the movement, but that this hadn't been used in the army for a long time.

The police then asked why an adjutant-chef on leave would be travelling around with a cord that hadn't been used for several years for training commandos? Chanal replied that he often used his van to 'store stuff' because he only had an NCO's room in his Fontainebleau barracks.

In the interview on 11 August, Chanal was questioned once again about his movements around the time of Trevor's death. He was asked about the spade found in his van, where did it come from? He replied that he had bought it in the winter of 1984-85. He said he last used it in Normandy between the 19th and 21st August.

He was asked about a substantial withdrawal of money he had made, of 2,500 francs, on 1st August and he declared he had taken the money out of the Crédit Agricole in Mourmelon. [This was significant, as it definitely located Chanal in Mourmelon on 1 August. In previous interviews he had said he was in Verdun or Normandy on this date.] He was also asked about his whereabouts from the 1st to 9th August 1987. He replied he had gone to the parachute club in Mourmelon on the 1st and 2nd August but that he couldn't remember if he made any jumps because he didn't note anything on his parachute record book during the month of August 1987. He repeated that he left Mourmelon on the 3rd of August for Verdun.

'On the 4th August I continued touring (Verdun) and I started to use my video camera because it was fine. I can't tell you exactly what I visited during that day. The same goes for the 5th of August. I think I spent the night of the 4th/5th on the carpark either at Douaumont Fort or the Fort of Vaux. In any case I am categorical that it was on the Verdun site. I toured alone at all times except for the guided visits. I always slept alone in my camping-car. At no time, since I left Mourmelon, did I pick up a hitchhiker. I don't remember seeing any.'

He was asked: 'Can you give an explanation as to the discovery of baggage and camping equipment 3 kilometres away from the place you were, camping gear belonging to a young hitchhiker found dead?'

Chanal was resolute: 'I can't give any answer as I have nothing to do with their being dropped in the Haute-Marne area, near Lac Du Der.'

The police asked again: 'Did you, during the period from 1st to the 7th August pick up a young man from England?'

Chanal decided enough was enough: 'I won't answer any more questions.'

Later that same day, the police went back to Chanal to interview him once more. This time, he was not in the mood to cooperate at all. Their testimony simply states:

'At 15.00hrs, we interviewed Chanal again, and asked: To whom do the spade and the St Michael underpants found in your camping van belong?'

The interviewer noted that the interviewee withdrew into total silence.

While Chanal was in prison for the abduction and rape of Falvay, he was interrogated again about his movements between 1 and 9 August, 1987. He could not substantiate where he had been and at one stage he even admitted he left Mourmelon for Fontainebleau and not Verdun on 3 August. It was also discovered that while Chanal was registered as having been at the Mourmelon club on Saturday 1 August, there was no sign of him being there on Sunday 2nd. His explanation was that he had simply gone back to Fontainebleau. However, his mileage for that first week of August, 1987 was a colossal 1215km, which would have suggested that he had undertaken much longer journeys than he was admitting to. If this was the case, then it was looking highly likely that Pierre Chanal was on the road at the same time Trevor was hitchhiking from Poligny to Calais via Reims and Saint-Quentin, although they would have been going in opposite directions.

His and Trevor's paths could have crossed at any of four times between Chalons-sur-Marne and Reims on that fateful day, 3 August, 1987.

The investigating file on Trevor's murder showed that, as well as taking out a large sum of money on 1 August, Chanal had also bought a lot of diesel for his van, for which he paid by cheque. The van was old and used up a lot of diesel and oil, so he went through a lot of cheques. Jean Du Pont, one of the original founders of the 'Disappeared of Mourmelon' group, had done a lot of detective work on Chanal's movements and the garage cheques helped to map out the routes he took on any given trip. Also, on the back of each cheque, Chanal had written the mileage. These cheques could link Chanal to a route that tied him to Trevor's murder. However, the cheques, although noted in the file, went missing early in the investigation and Judge Marien said he had never seen them. Where were they?

As I read the file, I was struck once again by the fact that, during the time it was being put together, the late 1980s, I was on my own, piecing together the scant news reports I was getting from Caroline and Noeleen. No official came near me with any news. Even though at the time I instinctively felt Chanal was connected to Trevor's murder, I just didn't know how. His conviction for the abduction and rape of Palazs Falvay brought him to public attention and public scrutiny. Soon it would be the experts, along with the police and investigating magistrate, who would uncover Chanal's sinister past and finally bring him to justice. Or so I thought.

The file offered as many questions as it did answers. These questions would be the basis for Eric Dupond-Moretti's case to make sure Chanal would be indicted for Trevor's murder.

The most damning evidence against Chanal came from Palazs Falvay's sworn statement of 10 August, 1988, in which he detailed the torture he had undergone at the hands of the decorated army sergeant.

Palazs Falvay came to France in July 1988. A student from Budapest in Hungary, he had embarked on a hitchhiking holiday, arriving in France from Saarbrücken on 6 July. He was given a lift to the northern French cathedral city of Reims by a German motorist, before travelling to Paris where he stayed with a friend. By 7 August he decided to leave Paris and travel south, again hitch-hiking along the way. On 8 August he was at the Chalon-Nord exit of the motorway and trying to hitch a lift when a green van passed by. The driver was on his own and seemed to be singing. Palazs laughed when he saw him do this. It was about 7pm. The van driver did a turn just before the toll station and drove off. Much later, at around 10pm, the driver returned and this time stopped in front of the young student who asked if he was going south to Lyon. He nodded yes and Palazs got into the passenger seat of the van. They had no common language. The man drove very slowly on the motorway, about 60 km/h. Soon the van drove off the motorway and onto a trunk road. Palazs did not know where he was going and didn't care so long as he got to Lyon. The man did not speak during the journey but seemed nervous. He didn't look at Falvay but whistled tunes as they went along. Beyond the town of Macon, Falvay noticed that the man was no longer driving towards Lyon. They were in a place with few lights and stopped at a lonely junction that was dark. In the van, the man searched for a map and started to behave strangely. He gave Falvay an apple, then asked for a pen and appeared as if he were lost. Three or four times he got out of the van, climbed into the back to get something, a lamp, a map, an apple. The van stopped again, the man got out and into the back. Suddenly Falvay felt a strap pass around his neck, tighten very violently and pull his head backwards. Having secured the student, the man put Falvay's rucksack on the passenger seat and with another strap tied the young man's legs very tightly. Then the man, Pierre Chanal, pushed him forcibly onto the bed in the back of the van. Falvay described his attacker as acting like he was mad: his eyes were popping out of his head. Falvay was terrified that Chanal was going to kill him. It was then the abuse started and continued into the next day. At one point Chanal chained Falvay by an expertly arranged contraption which rendered him incapacitated and allowed Chanal to further abuse him. Some of the abuse was filmed by Chanal who Falvay recalled was very calm as he went about the filming. However there were times when he would fly into a rage, become agitated and furious again, on the verge of hysteria, shouting violently. Falvay didn't doubt that had the police not intervened, he would have been murdered. Chanal had already half strangled Falvay with a carefully knotted bootlace.

What went through my head as I read this, I can't remember because I've always tried to block it out, deny it, believe it wasn't true. I know I had nightmares afterwards, wondering if this had also happened to my son. I sometimes still do. I couldn't bear to tell my family, my other kids, what I'd read. Noeleen knew but even then I couldn't talk about it. Only one person knew the real truth about what had hapend to Trevor, and that was Pierre Chanal. I was determined to get the truth from him. I had to know for sure.

As far as I was concerned, all the evidence pointed to Pierre Chanal as my son's murderer. While he was currently in prison for the abduction and rape of Palazs Falvay, under French law he would be eligible for early release after six years of his ten-year sentence. Since he had been in custody since 1988, this meant that he could apply for release from the end of 1994. All we had to do was keep him in prison long enough to build a case against him. Although he had already been indicted for Trevor's murder, in French law one could be charged with a crime but not brought to court until there was enough evidence. This evidence had to be deemed sufficient, first by the investigating magistrate, then by the state prosecutor. Eric believed that there were striking similarities between the Falvay case and Trevor's, and that Chanal was responsible for both crimes. He was determined to have the similarities in the file on the criminal case that lead to Chanal's imprisonment investigated again in relation to Trevor's case. It was, therefore essential that we keep Chanal in prison while we built a strong case, linking both cases, to get him into court and on trial for Trevor's murder.

CHAPTER 7

Face to Face with Chanal

On 31 January 1995, Pierre Chanal submitted a request for release from prison. I had only ten days in which to lodge a counter-appeal to have him remain in prison. I had to drop everything at home and work fast. I would have to get to France and be seen to be in court.

Judge Marien had written to Eric telling him that Chanal was making an appeal for early release. The judge gave details of the time and date of the appeal and the court in which it would take place. Judge Marien also sent a set of documents directly to me that I was to sign immediately and post on to Eric so that he could lodge our counter-appeal as soon as possible at the court where the appeal would be heard. We had to hope that the post was on time, as any delay at all could mean we would miss our ten-day window and Chanal would walk free.

Eric told me it was important for me to be seen in court, even though I wasn't actually summonsed to be there. He also insisted I make maximum use of the media. He would be making all the arguments against why Chanal should be released but I would have to have a presence there and would be required to make statements to the press. However there was one most important caveat: I was not allowed, under any circumstances, to accuse Chanal publicly of anything. In fact, it would be better to not even mention his name.

I was now being asked to talk about the case to anyone who would listen but not to mention the main suspect. I could not afford to accuse Chanal in public. It was up to the court to do that. Even Dominique would say to me, 'Eroline, you have to be quiet,' which was the last thing you'd expect a journalist to say to you!

So, while Eric insisted I go public with Trevor's case, I was not allowed to mention Chanal in connection with it. How on earth was I going to manage this challenge? It seemed impossible.

During the trial of Chanal for the abduction of Palazs Falvay, a laser test of molecules carried out by the University of Metz positively identified a hair found in Chanal's van as being that of Patrick Gache, the eighteen-year-old army conscript who had disappeared on 30 April, 1987, the same year as Trevor was murdered.

On the strength of this information, in June 1992 the investigating magistrate at Chalons-sur-Marne, Murielle Fusina, who held the brief for six of the seven Mourmelon victims, had charged Chanal with their imprisonment and assassination. This was the case where we had first encountered Dominique Rizet, but it was only now drawing to a close.

The case was weakened by the absence of bodies, and the identification of the Gache hair sample was not enough on its own to convict Chanal. The soldiers' families tried to have the case of the seventh missing soldier, Patrice Dubois, which was being handled by an investigating magistrate in Troyes, transferred to Chalons. Trevor's case would make their cases stronger again, yet his case was currently with Judge Marien in Saint-Quentin. Logically, it would make sense to have all the cases grouped together under the one investigating magistrate. Madame Fusina indicated that her evidence would be insufficient to keep Chanal in prison beyond 15 December 1994, when he would be due for conditional release.

At Reims Appeal Court in August 1994, the charges against Chanal in the Mourmelon cases were lifted. This was a devastating blow to the families of the young conscripts, who were convinced that Chanal had been responsible for the disappearance and probable murder of their sons. Some of the families had been asking questions about their sons' disappearance for over a decade. Chanal was the only suspect. A lot now hung on our counter-appeal. If we could keep Chanal in jail, it would strengthen our case to have him charged with Trevor's murder. If we were successful with our case, then there could be an argument for having the other 'Disappeared' cases re-opened and examined properly. We needed to win this counter-appeal.

We had a challenge on our hands, and, as usual, we needed money to pay for it. Noeleen decided to talk to Aer Lingus and see what they could do for us. She told them what we were doing. To our surprise and relief, she managed to get us a flat rate of payment even if we were to stay over a weekend. Next it was my turn to soften our landing with a visit to the Credit Union. I couldn't risk telling them the truth about why I needed a loan, so I said I was doing house improvements. Over the next decade, I went back to the Credit Union many times asking for the same loan for house improvements. As the years wore on, I often wondered whether I should change this explanation, as I couldn't possibly improve my house any further. But each time I made the request, it was granted so I stuck with it. Thank God they never asked to see the house!

I researched how much it would cost to have an interpreter in court with me for the appeal. They charged a staggering £35 an hour and I would have needed one for at least twelve hours at a time, since an appeal could go on all day. I contacted the Department of Foreign Affairs for their help but they wrote to tell me that the affair was outside of their remit. Elizabeth McCullough, the Second Secretary in Paris, had been very helpful over the years and was very sympathetic, but the department could not provide translators for court, except in the case of a trial.

There was no way I could afford the interpreting fees on my own, so Eric and I came up with a plan. But in order for it to work, I had to trust him completely.

In the meantime I took up French at night classes so I could at least try and make a stab at understanding for myself what was going on. I was truly terrible, and in terms of my French language education, I could say I never really made it out of baby infants!

The day before the appeal, Noeleen and I packed our bags and flew from Dublin to Paris and hired a car. We arrived in Amiens an hour or so later, but because of the one-way street system, we had no idea where we were going or how to get around. I tried my brand new French out on a postman and asked for directions to the court and our hotel. To our utter amazement, he put his bag into our car, told Noeleen to move over in the driver's seat as he got in and started the car. He then drove us to the court to show us where it was, then onto the hotel we were staying in. He even parked the car for us. He had no English at all but, as well as my woeful French, I had the letter indicating where we needed to go, and that, thank goodness, was enough for him.

Once established in the hotel, we went back again to find the court so that we would have our route planned for the next day. If we were even a little late, we wouldn't get into court and the whole point of us being there would be a waste. We could miss the proceedings and Chanal could walk free.

I followed Noeleen. She would say, 'do you think this is the right way?' and I'd just say, 'yes, I think so' so that she wouldn't think I was completely useless. A few times, I would recognise where we were. We walked for miles.

The morning arrived and Noeleen and I made our way to the court. We went early and hung around the gates to see if we could catch a glimpse of Chanal in the police van. I had never seen him in the flesh and wanted to get a look at him before I came face to face with him in court. We didn't see him. In fact, they had already brought him into the building through a back door.

The appeal was to be a private affair, which surprised me a little, because I had always assumed all court appearances were public. No one was allowed into the court except my lawyer, Eric, Chanal, his lawyer, some policemen, the judges and me. Noeleen had to stay outside. I looked around for anyone who had come in support of Chanal. I knew Dominique had met with his sister and mother and that he came from a very large family – fifteen children in all. Yet none of his family turned up to support him. Maybe they were embarrassed, I thought. One thing I was certain about, I was glad he wasn't my son.

I had imagined a grand old ostentatious courtroom with legions of lawyers, Chanal in the dock and the rest of us prepared to take the stand as the public looked on from a gallery above us. Mind you, all I had in the way of court experience was watching too many courtroom dramas on television. Instead the room was surprisingly tiny and ordinary, only just big enough for our group. There were three black-robed judges who sat in front of a long bench. A court stenographer took notes, and about three or four armed police were stationed at the back of the room. Noeleen had taken up a prime position at the top of the steps just outside the courtroom. She had managed to bring in her camera, which was not usually allowed. She had shown it to a policeman on her way in through the lobby and he knew what she intended to do with it but had not stopped her. She felt that he might even have winked at her. As Chanal descended the stairs, Noeleen stepped out in front of him and quickly took a photo. He was not at all pleased and raised his hand as if to hit her, but she stood her ground and got her picture.

Meanwhile I was inside, waiting to come face to face for the first time with my son's killer. The police searched my bag and pockets, then took my bag away and left it at the end of my seat. I wondered if they thought I might pull a gun on Chanal or try to stab him. I won't deny the thought didn't cross my mind. But I was calm and collected, for now.

A gaunt, sick looking man appeared. He seemed to have enormous, evil looking eyes. It was Chanal. I expected him to be much bigger and more powerful, but he wasn't at all. He wore a blue tracksuit. I noticed that his wrists were bandaged and he seemed sedated. I had heard on the way into court that he had tried to commit suicide in his cell in Alsace the day before by cutting his wrists with a smuggled razor.

Chanal kept swallowing as if his throat was dry. He moved into our bench with his lawyer, Pierre Gonzalez de Gaspard. Eric sat next to him, then me. I was literally at arm's length from him. If I leaned back slightly, I got the best view of him.

I couldn't take my eyes off him. This was probably the last person Trevor saw before he died. What did he say to Trevor, what did Trevor say to him? Did Trevor know he was in danger? Did he put up a fight? What had this man done to my child? The police removed chains that tied his bandaged hands to his feet.

Eric got up and argued as to why Chanal should not be released. Eric was a big grizzly bear of a man, prepossessing and tenacious. He spoke in rapid French, barking his points at the judges' bench. Then Eric put our 'interpreting' strategy into action. When he finished talking, he sat down next to me and whispered in my ear as if he was translating everything into English for me so that I would know everything that was being said. I nodded sagely, saying 'Yes, yes' as if understanding and taking on board every point. Then I whispered to him and he too would nod and agree in English. This was the pretence we had worked out to cover the fact that I could not pay for a translator. We maintained the strategy throughout the appeal and it seemed to have fooled everybody.

Days before the appeal, Eric had explained exactly what would happen at each point in the proceedings so I felt like I had been in rehearsals for today's performance. What was the point of it? Well, for one thing, there was no way I was going to let Chanal think I didn't understand what was going on. I meant business, I was determined to make sure he would stay behind bars and I would have done anything Eric had asked me if I thought it would help our case. I didn't want to look stupid. As it happened, I became very good at reading body language. I would watch intently every move, grimace and scowl that Eric would make and almost know what he was talking about.

I would know if things were going well, or if they were not.

Both Eric and Gaspard severely criticised how long the case had lain dormant and complained that a breakdown in the justice system had blocked any progress in the case for eight years. This was the only point on which both men were to agree.

Eric fixed the judges in his sights and launched his arguments to keep Chanal in prison. Pierre Chanal should not be released. There were striking similarities between Trevor's case and that of the Hungarian boy, Falvay. The autopsy on Trevor's body had mentioned a strangulation wound of 8mm wide. Eric said, 'We know from the Hungarian case that Chanal used straps on him, so why has no effort been made to see if the straps found in the van correspond to the wound? We need further investigation.'

He went on to point out that the soil samples taken from the place Trevor was buried matched those on a spade found in Chanal's van. He then argued that the route Chanal took in his camper van corresponded with Trevor's hitchhiking route home and where his rucksack was found in Lac Du Der. He could prove that Chanal was in the Lac Du Der area at that time. Warming to his theme, Eric rose to his feet as he demanded that I be allowed to see the clothes seized by police from Chanal's van and quarters so as to identify whether any belonged to Trevor. In particular he argued that I be allowed to check if one of the many pairs of underpants recovered from Chanal's van belonged to Trevor.

Eric was doing well. The judges listened intently to his arguments. I felt we had a chance to win here and keep Chanal in prison.

Pierre Gonzalez de Gaspard was Chanal's lawyer and he was a striking, flamboyant figure, small with jet-black hair and a pointed but pleasant face. He reminded me of the famous French chanteur Charles Aznavour, but with a biting incisive wit. He was one of the most notable lawyers in France and, so I was told, conducted his business from behind a colossal antique table in a gilt-edged palatial office on the Champs-Élysées in Paris. I looked at Eric, who was larger, bearded, less sophisticated and who seemed fidgety by comparison. Gaspard swept to the floor. He was most impressive. He argued that, legally, there were no grounds for Chanal's release to be hampered, that such a time had elapsed that it was unreasonable to charge this man with one murder after he had spent so much time in prison for something else. It was the sort of legal argument you would hear in a courtroom drama that would get the defendant off.

I felt my confidence in our win melt away. The judges were now listening intently to his arguments. Would Chanal walk free after all?

For four hours the arguments went back and forth. I tried to follow the action as much as I could. While both Eric and Gaspard gave great performances, the judges' expressions were inscrutable. I had no idea what they might be thinking. However, the longer it went on, the happier I felt that at least we were getting a good hearing. At one point, Eric was called up to the judges' bench and there was much whispering. With relief, I realised it was only a short break in proceedings and that they would be continuing. And so the arguments raged again between Eric and Gaspard. Gaspard seemed much more commanding and in control. As the hours drew on, I became less convinced we were doing well. Of course, I had nothing to base it on except instinct. I hoped I would be proven wrong. During the whole proceedings Chanal kept his gaze focused straight ahead.

And then the talking was over. I found Noeleen in the corridor and we waited for what seemed an eternity for a decision. Eventually I was called back in. Noeleen and I hugged briefly before I returned to my bench. The judges announced their decision.

Chanal would stay in jail. The judges wanted further investigation between the soil samples found on Chanal's spade and where Trevor was buried. Chanal had lost his appeal and we had got our first victory. Eric's arguments had won the day. For the first time in years I allowed myself to be happy and rejoice at the news. I was doubly excited because I believed that if the judges ruled that Chanal should not be released because of the strength of Eric's arguments, then it would only be a matter of time before Chanal would be charged with Trevor's murder and would finally be tried. I looked forward to my day in court.

I came out of the court looking for Noeleen and to pass on the great news. Instead I walked into a wall of journalists and television crews; there were at least a hundred people in front of us. Eric took my arm and guided me along. We were mobbed. People, cameras, sound booms and microphones surrounded us and pushed and shoved at us. I have no idea what I said or what Eric said – we both answered whatever questions came at us, but afterwards he kept me moving towards our car. Eventually we caught up with Noeleen and all of us bundled into the car and raced off. As we looked behind us, journalists were running down the street after us. I'd never seen anything like it.

In the back of the car, we were jubilant. Noeleen told me how she had sat outside the courtroom with Gaspard's son who had driven him to the court. She had just heard our news. As journalists swarmed around Eric and me, Gaspard had come up to her and shook hands and said 'How is your sister?' Noeleen smiled back at him, 'I sat all morning here with your son,' she replied, 'and if your beautiful son was murdered, how would you be today?' He put his arm around her and gave her a hug. 'You're great women,' he said.

I was barely back home in Naas when I got the call again from Eric. Chanal had made another appeal for release. We would have to go to court again. It was now March 1995.

This time around, myself and Noeleen were getting a bit more organised and experienced in handling the media. The case was attracting a growing amount of coverage at home, but mostly in France. I was doing interviews with newspapers almost every week and both Dominique and Caroline were sending me videotapes of news reports and documentaries that were running on all the French television channels. This was one of the biggest murder stories of the century and it seemed people could not get enough of what was happening. For me, though, it was all about keeping the pressure up on Chanal, keeping him in jail.

As the appeal approached, I went back to France with Noeleen. We met Dominique Rizet. On the day of the appeal there were television cameras everywhere and crews from almost every country, or so it seemed. Certainly from all over France as well as Belgium and Germany. There were huge gatherings of journalists waiting outside the court. More and more newspapers picked up on the story every day.

I was totally amazed that there was so much interest in the case and the appeal. I had no idea just how big a story it was in France. Noeleen and I would be walking past newspapers that had a picture of me opposite a picture of Chanal and in huge bold type the headline would read 'A Mother Against Chanal'. The interest wasn't so much in Trevor or his case per se, it was Chanal and all the young French boys who had disappeared and who had probably been murdered by him. Chanal was the chief suspect and their cases had yet to be dealt with. The issue was building to a national scandal.

Noeleen and myself went to the court in Amiens early. We had had enough of cameras and were delighted that we approached the building unfettered by television crews. As we slipped through the door to the courtroom, Noeleen remarked, 'isn't it great, we've missed them'. Just then we went through a further set of glass swing doors only to be confronted by a whole battalion of journalists. They had been waiting inside for us all along and had caught our every move on our way in, filming us the whole way from the entrance into the court.

I had to push my way through while Noeleen had to wait outside. I took up my seat on the same bench as last time. I was keen to see what state Chanal might be in when he arrived. He was much more alert than on the previous outing. I thought he also looked a bit stronger, better fed even than before, dressed in jeans and a jacket. He looks like he's being looked after, I said to myself, disappointed. Unlike the first appeal, I found him looking at me occasionally, though his expression gave nothing away. Sometimes he would a crane his head back, stretching his neck, as if he were trying to break free of something. It looked like a nervous tic. I hoped he was nervous. When he looked at me again, I returned his stare with what I hoped was a resolute expression. But inside my head was turmoil. I had a hundred questions for him to answer. They were always the same questions. He was probably the last person Trevor had ever spoken to. What did Trevor say to him, what did he say to Trevor? What did he do to my beautiful son?

The police had said that Trevor had died very quickly but Eric told me that this was unlikely to have been the case, given the experience of Palazs Falvay. Over and over again, I asked myself, did Chanal make Trevor suffer, and for how long? The only way I would ever find out was if Chanal confessed. Would it happen? I doubted it but I lived in hope.

The judges called for order and the appeal got under way. I was getting better at picking up what was being said. I knew the words now for soil samples and underpants. I knew when they had moved onto a different argument. I watched the judges' faces and if they didn't argue back with Eric then I knew they had accepted a point and that was good. If Eric argued with them, but was smiling at the end of it, then that too was good. Eric argued that he could prove that Chanal was in the Lac Du Der area around the time Trevor was murdered and his rucksack discarded. There was a parachute club there and Chanal was not only a member but had been using it then. It was proof that Chanal could be linked to Trevor's murder, but would it be enough to convince the judges?

Gaspard took to the floor, as impressive as before. My heart sank. He argued in his defence of Chanal that, as a human being, Chanal had a right to be released, having served his time.

Three hours later, the arguments came to an end. The judges conferred and announced their decision. Just keep him in jail, I prayed, just keep him in jail. Eric put his arm around me, 'He stays in jail,' he said.

As Chanal was led away from our seat, he stopped alongside me. 'Madame O'Keeffe,' he said, '*Je suis innocent*.' I needed no translation. A chill shuddered through my body. I looked him in the eye but said nothing. 'Come on, Eroline,' said Eric and ushered me out.

When the court finished, Noeleen and I tried to evade the journalists. We beetled off down a corridor, looking for a toilet from which to climb out the window. Unfortunately, none was big enough but we waited a long time before leaving, hoping they would get bored and go home. The next day, Noeleen and I were crossing the road in Paris and were amazed when a man came up to us and put his arm around me and said, 'Well done, well done, France is so proud of you.'

In May, yet another appeal for release was lodged by Chanal. Again Eric got in touch with me and I counter-lodged an appeal to have Chanal kept in prison. Again I had ten days to get organised before Chanal appeared in court. Could we be lucky a third time?

Dominique organised a press conference in the hotel where we were staying. We had never been to a press conference, let alone become the subject of one. In front of me was a sea of people and television cameras, at least a hundred bodies. A lot of the journalists spoke English and they would ask, 'Madame O'Keeffe, what do you think?' 'Tell us about Chanal.' I said nothing. I was under strict orders from Eric not to say a thing in case I prejudiced Trevor's case by saying the wrong thing. In particular I was not to accuse Chanal and that was the main thing. I just concentrated on keeping my mouth shut, which, it has to be said, is a difficult thing for me to do at any time. So many people would say to me, 'Chanal is guilty.' The guards on the door would say it; Eric believed it and we even thought that Gaspard probably believed it but I could not say it. I found it so hard to say nothing, not to accuse him, to never let it slip, never let my guard down. Eric did all the talking, answering all the journalists' questions with the ease of a seasoned performer. I could not have been happier that he was our lawyer.

The next day we arrived at court, this time in Chalons-sur-Marne rather than Amiens. Judge Marien was the presiding judge. I was getting used to being in court but each appeal brought its own store of worry: would our luck run out, would we lose this time, would Chanal be freed? Noeleen had to wait outside as usual. Inside, I took up my seat beside Eric and waited for Chanal to arrive. The first thing I noticed was that Pierre Gaspard was not with him. In his place was a new figure – André Buffard – a stout, jowly chap who in no way commanded the room as Pierre Gaspard had done. It seemed that Chanal had a new lawyer. I was delighted. I'd always felt Gaspard was such a strong opponent that we would run out of our luck one day and he'd win the appeal for Chanal. I sat back in my seat and allowed myself to get comfortable. As soon as I heard Buffard's voice, so much softer and weaker than his flamboyant predecessor, I thought, wonderful, Chanal hasn't a hope with this guy. Of course, I had nothing to base this supposition on, except the man's demeanour. I learnt afterwards that his arguments were as cogent as Gaspard's except that Buffard had a lighter voice and very different style of presentation. There was not the same force or tension between Eric and Chanal's new lawyer. I felt the combat was one-sided, and we were looking stronger.

However, unlike Gaspard, Chanal's new lawyer didn't look at me when he mentioned me to the court. It was a small gesture but it made me nervous. I had always liked the fact that Gaspard was civil, even friendly, to Noeleen and me. He had once mentioned that he 'did what he was paid to do' and so I fully believed that if circumstances were different he would be on our side, not Chanal's. True or not, in the previous appeals this thought sustained me every time I heard Gaspard make a great imposing point.

However in this third appeal, my early confidence that we could have an easy win was ebbing away. This new lawyer, even with his quiet voice, was showing real intent. He could win the appeal and Chanal would walk.

Three, or maybe four hours later, the arguments were wound up and the judges made their decision. Chanal would stay in prison. He had failed three times to get his release. I was so relieved. However I knew this wasn't the end of it and that he would make another appeal, and possibly just keep going until his sentence was up. But I was ready to take him on; mentally I was prepared to fight against every appeal he would make. Yes, I was ready for him all right.

In May 1995, I finally got the call to see Judge Marien and was to be allowed to see Chanal's belongings. The sum total of what I was to look at was brought out in a plastic bag. In it were underpants, loads of them. Each pair was sealed in a small plastic bag with a little red seal. Each bag was opened in turn and the underpants taken out and shown to me. There were thirty-two pairs in all. I recognised one of them as definitely belonging to Trevor. They were a small size St Michael brand, white with a red stripe, which I had bought for him before he went away. Later, Judge Marien would try to say that I had identified another pair, which were much larger and baggy, as being Trevor's. But I know I didn't. I was sure which underpants had belonged to my son. Not only had it been me who had bought them as a set for Trevor, but I also had the matching ones at home in Naas. I believed that the underpants Trevor was wearing when he was found were not his; they were French, the wrong size, and he had had enough underwear with him that he didn't need to buy any more in any event.

In that chilling moment I realised that Chanal was, without doubt, the murderer. All of these underpants had been retrieved from his van following his arrest for the abduction and rape of Palazs Falvay. It was as if Chanal had kept them as trophies. And my son's were amongst them. Oh dear God, let this just be a nightmare, I prayed. I knew then that Trevor had probably suffered the same fate, and worse, because he had been murdered after his ordeal. I felt beaten. The same waking nightmare returned: that I hadn't been there for him, hadn't been there to prevent my beautiful son from dying in – I couldn't bear to think about it – in such a miserable and cruel way. I felt a stinging physical pain. And it wasn't over. Next I had to identify a beige hand towel, which was one of two I had given Trevor before he left. I had bought them specially, and again had the third towel from the set at home in Naas.

For the moment, my whole being was concentrated on the work in front of me, identifying my son's belongings, the very basic stuff of normal everyday hygiene: towels and underwear.

When I left Judge Marien after that terrible meeting he told me that he would never release Chanal early; that he would serve his time. Foolishly, I believed him.

All through that night, the day's events replayed in my head. I now knew that Chanal had murdered my son. And my mind was filled with thoughts of what horror this monster might have put my young son through before he killed him. I had nightmares, still do, about the dreadful depravations, humiliations and pain that Chanal could have inflicted on Trevor over the hours he had him held hostage.

A month later, I was at home when I received a letter from the

French Embassy in Dublin telling me that there was a document for me at the embassy and that I would have to go to Dublin to collect it in person. The letter said I should make an appointment first. It all seemed overly officious, which made me a bit nervous. Briefly, I wondered if this could be a letter telling me that Chanal had made another appeal for release, but I dismissed the thought. After all, the judge had always sent those letters directly to Eric Dupond-Moretti. Why would he change now, and without telling me? I called the embassy and made my appointment but it was three or four days later when I drove up to Dublin, where I sat in a queue until it was my turn to go up to the desk. I was handed a letter. I looked at it and stopped short. I had seen this type of letter before. It was the same type that Judge Marien had sent to Eric three times before to let us know that Chanal had made an appeal for release.

As soon as I could, I found a phone and called Eric. He knew nothing of the appeal. In the past, this letter of notification had been sent to Eric, who then got in touch with me and, on my behalf, he made a counter-appeal within the ten-day timeframe. However, this time the notification came via the French Embassy in Dublin, Eric knew nothing of it and so our ten-day window had already been eaten into. Eric could do nothing until I had signed the letter and returned it to him. With a shaking hand, I signed the documents and sent them by registered post to Eric. A week later, Eric received my registered letter. It was too late. Two doctors had carried out a psychological assessment of Chanal and concluded that he was capable of being reintegrated into society. Judge Marien supported this. The ten days had elapsed and I knew what would happen. I felt sick.

I woke up to the sound of the telephone ringing. It was about 6 o'clock in the morning. Noeleen was on the line. 'Chanal is free. He was released this morning, an hour ago. I've just heard it on the radio.' The date was 19 June 1995. Chanal had finally succeeded.

I was beside myself with rage. I couldn't understand why the same magistrate who had always followed the same course of action in the succession of appeals lodged by Chanal – sending the documents to Eric, then onto me – had suddenly decided to send them instead to the French Embassy in Dublin? We found out that the judge had simply changed the system of how he notified people and didn't tell Eric or me in advance of Chanal's fourth appeal. And this was the same judge who had so recently told me that he would not release Chanal early; that he would serve his time. I couldn't understand it at all. I called the judge every name I could think of and some I had no idea what they meant. I felt he was nothing short of a rotten bastard for what he did and it made me sick. I was also convinced that it was a tactic to keep me away from court. I had growing suspicions that Chanal was being protected because of his high standing in the army. This just proved to me how true it was.

Noeleen was more pragmatic, 'We can't dwell on this or we'll get stuck. This is not the end,' she said, 'we have to plan our next move.'

I knew my next move. I decided to buy a gun.

CHAPTER 8

Portrait of a Murderer

I first came across the name of Pierre Chanal when I read about his arrest for the abduction of the Hungarian boy, Palazs Falvay. He would have been about forty-two going on forty-three then.

The French media were already linking his name with Trevor's murder. He was a former commando who had risen up through the ranks to warrant officer or sergeant-major in the crack 4th Dragoons regiment based in Fontainebleau military base. According to comrades he was 'an archetypal warrior and a man of steel'. He had served in Beirut at the height of the bloody civil war. Even the Irish newspapers had picked up on the story, referring to Chanal as a 'Rambo-style' figure and 'Rambo-Sadist'.

When he was arrested and interrogated for the abduction and rape of Palazs Falvay, he said that he and Falvay had engaged in rough sex but that it was consensual. However, police then questioned him about the disappearances of other young men in the area known as 'The Triangle of Death' and they also questioned him about Trevor's murder.

Chanal did not make life easy for the police. After his initial statements he decided to stop cooperating with the police and in reply to police questions he gave only his name, rank and serial number. He also repeated, like a mantra, the text of the Geneva Convention on the rights of prisoners of war. He had trained as a paratrooper and even had a certificate for his ability to resist under interrogation.

He was deemed a 'hard nut to crack'.

Born in St Etienne, on the road between Paris and Marseilles, and south of the commercial and industrial powerhouse of Lyon, Chanal was one of fifteen children, one of whom died in child-hood. He was fifth in the surviving family of seven boys and seven girls. The family was poor and Chanal never went much beyond primary education before going off to work in the steel industry in nearby Andrezieux. From there he decided to join the army and left home at a very young age, probably about fifteen or sixteen. As a boy he had reportedly lived in a shed at the bottom of the garden of the family home. He was a loner. His father, also Pierre, drank, and, I had heard from journalists covering the case, was possibly violent. His mother, Andrée, had her hands full with so many chil-dren to take care of.

Simone was his younger sister and the only one who gave Chanal any support during his time in prison and afterwards. She was also the only family member who turned up to give evidence during his trial in 2003.

Chanal lost contact with his parents almost from the time he left home; he hadn't spoken to his mother for several years and hadn't been in touch with other family members for at least seven-teen or eighteen years. When his father died he didn't even go home for the funeral.

The army became his family. He quickly moved up through the ranks, was universally acknowledged as a 'good soldier' and was decorated. He was made a sergeant in 1977. At this stage he was based in the Valdahon barracks in eastern France, but, following a training incident, where he fired live bullets over the heads of his terrified conscript charges, he was transferred to Mourmelon, further to the north. He was also accused of sexual harassment by a conscript in Valdahon. It's not clear if he suffered any further disciplinary action after this. However it was after his transfer that he cut off contact with his family and didn't even tell them that he had moved to Mourmelon.

In Mourmelon he was promoted to sergeant major (*adjutant-chef* in French terms) and put in charge of all disciplinary matters. As early as 1985 he was questioned about the disappearance of four young men from his battalion after the disappearance of civilian Patrice Denis in Chalons-en-Champagne. Thousands of troops from the garrison had been questioned in an exhaustive police trawl. Nothing had come of it except that, coincidentally or otherwise, Chanal was moved once again, this time from his base at Mourmelon to Fontainebleau barracks south of Paris in 1986. Despite the move to a new barracks, he still travelled north to Mourmelon every week to take part in skydiving jumps with his parachute club. He had been skydiving since 1977.

By the time he was arrested for the abduction of Palazs Falvay in 1988, Chanal was a high-ranking soldier, as well as a parachute instructor and was in charge of 270 conscripts.

On 10 August 1988, Chanal was taken in for questioning following the discovery of Palazs Falvay in the back of his van. One of the men asking the questions was policeman Jean-Marie Tarbes who had cause to be more than a little interested in this particular army man. For the past six years he had been investigating the disappearance of eight young men, but with no success in tracking down a perpetrator. Working on a gut instinct, the policeman started asking Chanal about the 1980-87 period. When detectives from Amiens also started asking him questions about Trevor's murder, Chanal was not prepared to play along and resisted questioning.

When I read the report of his interrogation, sometime in 1995, I was quite taken aback at how arrogant he appeared. Chanal claimed that the Hungarian hitchhiker had encouraged him and even wanted to be tied up. He said that, later, the young man stopped consenting to his behaviour, but he carried on anyway. 'If the foreigner had said no from the start, I wouldn't have forced him,' he declared.

Much later, while in prison, Chanal changed his mind completely and denied that he had sexual fantasies about making love to a bound partner. He stated that while in the three army camps he had no personal contact with any person outside work contacts. He made various claims about his sexual life, and how he had used prostitutes, though his statements varied as to whether he went to Paris to meet them or to Reims.

During his trial for the abduction and rape of Palazs Falvay, Chanal claimed that he had two girlfriends, one of whom said they had had a relationship, but not a sexual relationship. In 1992 and while Chanal was in prison, one of those alleged to have been a girlfriend came forward, saying that Chanal had told her he had killed the missing conscripts. She was now married with children but had been a barmaid in a pub used by army men in Mourmelon.

The woman said she had seen Chanal thirty times between September 1984 and August 1987. One night in 1986 she was waiting for a friend when Chanal turned up, covered in sweat, trembling and out of breath. 'I asked if he had a problem'. He replied, 'Leave me alone. I've done something stupid.' The following week when she saw him she claimed that she asked, 'Is it you, the people who've disappeared in Mourmelon?' He was perfectly calm as he replied, 'They'll have to prove it'. She then decided to provoke him; fuelled by drink and curiosity she lifted her skirt and sat on his lap. He had no physical reaction and told her he wasn't interested in women, he didn't like women.

She also claimed that, one day in early summer 1987, they were having coffee when he revealed: 'The first three who disappeared at Mourmelon, that was me.' In her statement she said, 'I was surprised, despite my suspicions, and I asked him, "Why are you telling me this?" "Because I trust you," he answered. She was horrified by what she was hearing but felt drawn to him and his strange personality. One of the last times she saw him was in August 1987, around the same time Trevor went missing. She claimed that she asked him about his victims and he told her that he took young lads who were hitchhiking by themselves. He got their confidence by talking to them. If they refused him, he beat them unconscious, then he tied their hands behind their backs. He waited until they woke up. She claimed that he told her: 'I sodomised them, then I killed them at the moment I climaxed.' When she asked him if he was not afraid he might get caught, he said simply, 'They will have to prove it to jail me.'

There was a lot of controversy about this statement and Chanal's lawyers argued that it was not credible and could not be admissible because it had come so late after the event. A fellow barmaid contradicted her further by saying the woman had only worked the bar for three days. Her account was never used as testimony in court, but it was made public in newspaper interviews with her.

The trial was to unearth a very sinister side to the highly decorated soldier and 'archetypal warrior and a man of steel'.

Some of the Mourmelon conscripts who served under Chanal were interviewed by police and I had access to their testimonies. They cited how cruel he could be. Comrades found him cold and withdrawn, a loner obsessed with fitness. Nobody ever heard him talk about his family, saw him receive letters, phone calls or visits.

Some of his colleagues would talk of how good he was as a soldier and leader.

The young conscripts who disappeared could all be connected in some way with Chanal. For example, Olivier Donner was gone from the barracks only a half hour when Chanal left, according to other lads in the same unit. Other recruits talked of how Chanal would sometimes call a boy back to sweep the floor when the others had gone, making him late for wherever he was going. On another occasion, Chanal deliberately kicked over a bucket of water and made one of the recruits stay behind to mop up. The recruit disappeared soon after.

In follow-up questioning years later, there were rolls and registers that Chanal was supposed to sign but didn't in the cases of the six missing conscripts from Mourmelon barracks. One of these registers recorded dental appointments, which Chanal would sign almost daily in 1981. However, he did not sign the dental register on 20 February, 1981, the day Serge Havet disappeared. He could not say how this happened. His signature was also missing for the days around the disappearance of Manuel Carvalho. Dates of

Chanal's leave seemed to coincide with the disappearance of some of the conscripts, for example, Olivier Donner and Patrick Gache.

Testimony was taken from young recruits who served under Chanal as well as from his own colleagues from the barracks in Mourmelon. The recruits in particular painted a picture of Chanal as a harsh and cruel teacher. Even some of the other officers were afraid of him.

Throughout all his questioning, Chanal strenuously denied any involvement in the disappearances of the young men, including Trevor. He always appeared to have an answer, even if it contradicted an earlier one. At one point, in one of his many interrogations, he was asked what was his problem with young soldiers, as he had been involved in so many incidents, including firing over the heads of conscripts, as well as numerous incidences of mistreatment.

'It's part of the military mentality,' he had answered glibly. 'If I had been at school with the Jesuits I probably wouldn't have done it.'

As well as being a committed and ruthless soldier, Chanal was renowned for the cleanliness of his quarters. His room was invariably the cleanest and tidiest in the block, though without books or personal mementos. His hobbies were also solitary – parachuting and flying microlight aircraft.

Years later, when Chanal had access to his file and could see that it was becoming clear that the foam mattress recovered from his van contained hairs from a number of people other than Chanal himself, he offered new information to try to explain away this evidence.

❑ ❑ ❑

Extract from Minutes of Interrogation of Pierre Chanal, 4/11/99.

Q: 'Your lawyer told us you wanted to give more details about the pieces of foam rubber found in your combi [van] and inside which numerous hair elements had been found. We are listening ...'

A: 'I found these pieces in a dump.'

Q: 'Where and when?'

A: 'It was after my transfer to Fontainebleau during the second term of 1986. It was in a dump, but I can't remember where exactly it was situated. Whether on the Mourmelon-Fontainebleau road or whether in a dump in the Mourmelon region, or in a dump in the Suippes region.'

Q: 'Do you usually salvage things in dumps?'

A: 'No, but I saw this piece of foam rubber by chance when passing by a dump.'

Q: 'Since you remember noticing this piece of foam rubber by chance, don't you think you should remember the place where you found it more precisely?'

A: 'No. I used to travel a lot along these routes.'

Q: 'Was it a big piece of foam rubber or several blocks of it?'

A: 'I took the pieces as they were. It was only dirty garbage.'

Q: 'According to your file, you would qualify as "Mr. Clean" and you declare yourself to be very aware of good hygiene. It doesn't tally with your dump story...'

A: 'These pieces of rubber foam were not soiled with mud. They were freshly abandoned. I can say that because they were clearly visible. Also, I put them in a cover.'

Q: 'Did anyone see you taking these pieces of rubber foam?'

A: 'I don't know.'

During his trial in 1989/90, Chanal was made to undergo psychological testing. FBI experts who examined the files of 230,000 sex crimes over ten years produced a psychological profile of sexual criminals that Chanal matched. Among the typical characteristics they noted were that he was obsessional, very cold, and had higher than average intelligence. The FBI specialists were almost certain of Chanal's guilt and reported that the motive for his criminal acts on young men, mainly conscripts, could date from his disciplinary transfer from Valdahon base to Mourmelon in 1977. Their report also stated that Chanal feared everything related to sex and could only have sexual relations with victims reduced to being powerless, over whom he had the power of life or death. Most importantly, the report said that only imprisonment or his own death would stop Chanal from killing again.

When I saw this report I thought, there is no way anyone is ever going to let this man back into the community. He is just too dangerous. How wrong I was.

The trial ended with Chanal being convicted of abduction and rape. He was sentenced to ten years in prison. He had served nearly half his sentence by the time I came face to face with him in court in 1995. He had had enough of prison. He wanted out.

He hated the captivity. Yet, apart from this loss of freedom, for Chanal, prison life was pretty similar to his life in the army. It was routine and disciplined. He had access to television and had a daily newspaper. I was appalled that he should have such luxuries and campaigned to have them removed from him. However he was put into isolation, for his own safety initially. He was an exemplary prisoner, as much as he had been an exemplary soldier. He probably thought if he behaved himself he could get out quicker.

He spent his days in furious bouts of rigorous exercise and long periods of intense concentration, staring at the walls of his cell for hours on end. When I heard this I wondered did he think of what he had done, did he feel remorse? I couldn't pity him. I wanted him tried for Trevor's murder, I wanted him convicted and never to be free again to do to anyone else what he had done to my son.

During the appeals I had located Chanal's sister's address and I wanted to go to her house and ask to speak to her. I wanted to know what she knew. Had he confided in her? Could she be persuaded to give evidence against him if she actually met one of her brother's victims families? Noeleen was worried that it might damage the case if we were seen to be talking to any of Chanal's family, and that we might go over ground that we shouldn't. I said, 'Sure no one will know me'. 'Are you joking?' Noeleen replied, 'Of course they will. There's been pictures of you all over the place; someone would recognise you. It's too risky.' As much as I wanted to know what the sister knew about her brother, Noeleen was right. It was too risky. I would just have to let it go.

It was telling that during the six years that Chanal was in prison, there were no further reported disappearances in the 'Triangle of Death'. No one went missing, no young men were abducted and no anguished parents were left behind to worry about where they might be, what might have happened to them. All in all, the Mourmelon area, and France for that matter, was a safer place without Pierre Chanal. This was the principal reason I felt we needed to keep him, at all costs, in prison.

When Chanal was released from prison, in June 1995, I wanted to kill him myself. I knew that he was going to live with his sister, Simone, in Saint-Just-Saint-Rampert, near where the family had grown up in Saint Etienne and south of Lyon. He had to report to the police and his driving licence was taken from him.

However the media soon found him and found stories to write about him. One such story involved Chanal's attempt to resume his parachute teaching after he was released from prison by joining a private club near his home. According to the report I read, Chanal was giving a one hundred-year-old woman parachute lessons. Mad enough that a one hundred-year-old woman would want to jump out of a plane with a parachute, but with Chanal as instructor? I actually laughed out loud when I read it. His time in the parachute club was, however, curtailed when his trainees and colleagues realised who he was and shunned him, forcing him to leave.

Over the next few years, newspaper journalists, television documentary makers and photographers would dog his every step and report everything he did. As time went on, he would be known in his own area and elsewhere and I know it got particularly embarrassing for him attempting to live amongst his townspeople. Little by little people in his area got to know who he was, they would see his picture in their local and national newspapers and on television. I've never counted myself much of a fan of the media but in this instance I applauded them their tenacity. In the absence of any judicial interrogation of Chanal, the media were the only people watching him, and in my view, this man needed close surveillance.

Much later, in September 2000 and under yet another cross-examination by the investigating magistrate, Chanal was to set out his own personal defence in a seven-point statement that would, as it turned out, be the nearest he would give as public testimony.

1. 'I wish to state again that I am totally innocent in this affair and the matters I'm said to be involved with, in spite of everything that has been said about me.

2. If Falvay had no traces of torture, it's because he was, I would say, 80% consenting and he was not tortured as it has been said.

3. It's true that we have mentioned a lot during these last two days that my sexual inclinations were unusual, essentially solitary, apart from the few relations I have had with a few persons. You understand that it has been very difficult for me to talk about this subject. To reveal myself as I have done has been for me very painful and a great shame at the same time.

4. I do not know to this day whether it is a case of missing persons or crimes, apart from the two victims whose bodies were found. Moreover it has not been possible to determine precisely on what date these people disappeared. It is not known that I was present when they disappeared. I add that nobody ever saw me with any one of these victims.

5. I'm told that when I'm around people disappear. I note that the dates of the so-called disappearances are irregular. And I repeat

Right: Eroline outside the police station in Saint-Quentin, France.

Below: Noeleen's daughter, Caroline, who also died in suspicious circumstances in France.

Bottom: (l to r): With Bill, our journalist friend Dominique Rizet, and my sister, Noeleen.

Left: Pierre Chanal in military uniform.

Bottom: Chanal is led in handcuffs to the courthouse.

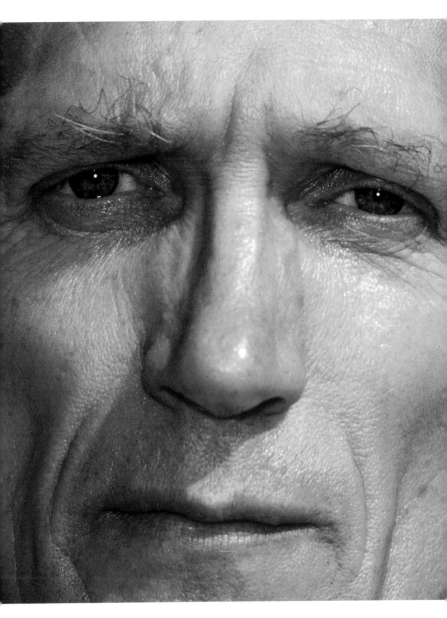

Above: Face to face with Pierre Chanal.

Left: Noeleen took this photo of Chanal on his way into the court of appeal.

Bottom: Surrounded by the press. We were amazed at the level of interest in the case.

Above: Evidence of a crime. A chain found in the back of Chanal's van after the abduction and rape of Hungarian hitchhiker Palazs Falvay.

Bottom: Chanal protests his innocence in a letter written before one of his suicide attempts.

J'accuse tous les faux témoins qui se sont déshonoré dans des déclarations calomnieuses, pourquoi ont-ils fait cela ?

A toute ma famille, à tous mes amis, à tous mes accusateurs je clame une dernière fois mon innocence.

Je Suis

INNOCENT !!!

INNOCENT !!!

INNOCENT !!!

D Kjul

STOP!
LOOK!
INJUSTICE

WE WANT CHANAL IN PRISON
UN'TILL PROVEN INNOCENT OF
TREVOR O'KEEFFE'S MURDER

YOUR SIGNATURE WILL HELP
GET : JUSTICE
FOR MY SON.
PLEASE SIGN:

ENQUETE

CRIMINELLE

Above: Our homemade poster pleading for signatures to a petition to keep Chanal in prison.

Opposite: With the photo I took of Trevor before he left on his travels.

Above: In court on the day of the trial of Pierre Chanal for Trevor's murder, 14 October 2003. (l to r): Noeleen (partly hidden). Nicole (interpreter), Judy, myself and Tootsie.

Bottom: The family, grown up. (l to r) James, Tootsie, William, Judy. We will never forget Trevor.

that I'm free for the past 5 years and that nobody has disappeared.

6. I've been questioned, I'm being questioned, witnesses are questioned about events that happened, in the case of the earliest ones, twenty years ago, and the last, thirteen years ago. Given that much, it is not abnormal that during questioning my memory is a little bit lacking, or even a lot.

7. I'm innocent, and that's all.'

CHAPTER 9

New Evidence, Old Heartache

Chanal was free. He had won his appeal in my absence and he was free. He was the most dangerous man in France and he was allowed to go free. The justice system had failed, as far as I was concerned and there was nothing else for it. I was going to shoot him myself. I knew where he lived and how to get to him. I felt it would be the only real justice he deserved. Noeleen talked to me for days to get me to see sense. We would talk all day and then I'd sit up all night thinking of how I could kill him. I just couldn't see another way out. Noeleen was there constantly. She was the good angel sitting on my shoulder, telling me the right thing to do. After some days, I listened.

I reluctantly agreed to give the courts one last chance. I rang Eric Dupond-Moretti, 'Is there anything else we can do?' I asked him. He told me that we could lodge a final appeal to have Chanal re-arrested if I initiated a private murder prosecution against him. 'OK, let's do it,' I said.

We waited for a date to appear in court.

Meanwhile Chanal was free. I had to concentrate very hard on trying to put him out of my mind. I got stuck into work.

Dominique Rizet sent me a documentary that had been made for French television and which had filmed Chanal free as he went about his daily business in the town of Saint-Just-Saint-Rampart where he was living with his sister. I had heard all sorts of stories about him but had not actually seen him since he was set free. I sat down on my own to watch it. I hadn't seen him for two years and I was shocked by what I saw.

The gaunt man I had witnessed in the court during the appeals had gone; instead he looked to be in the prime of health and was dressed in a navy blue overcoat, carrying a dandy little male handbag. He looked every inch the elegant gentleman. I knew that his army pension had been restored to him when he left prison, so obviously he was able to afford new clothes and was looking after himself. I just felt it wasn't right. I remembered how I had felt when I heard he had access to television and daily newspapers while in prison. I was disgusted that he should have these privileges, in fact, that he should have any privileges at all. I continued to watch, indignant yet aware of how powerless I was to do anything about it. The next film sequence made me really angry.

Incredibly, it showed that Chanal was back behind the steering wheel of a vehicle. Chanal's driving licence had been revoked yet he had obviously thought about how he might circumvent the order without breaking it and had resorted to driving around in a battery-operated car for which he would not need a licence. It was just like him, I thought, to be so cunning. What was to stop him going off and finding some young lad to molest? I thought. I couldn't understand how the authorities could let this man out onto the streets.

I had to do something to stop myself from going mad thinking about Chanal free and swanking around Saint Rampart in his fine navy coat. I called Noeleen and suggested we get a petition going. If we couldn't get the magistrate to listen to us, maybe we could get people behind us and go direct to the Minister for Justice. Anything was worth a shot. The *Irish Star* newspaper approached me and asked if they could back us and help organise a petition in Ireland for signatures to be presented to Foreign Affairs to get Chanal re-arrested and quickly brought to trial for the murder of Trevor O'Keeffe.

As well as getting signatures from people all over Ireland through the newspaper, we also took the campaign to France. We made placards with a picture of Trevor and details of his murder written below. We got A4 sheets printed up with, at the top, the picture of Trevor that I had taken in his beanie hat and gear as he set out for England, and at the bottom, a picture of Chanal that we found in a newspaper. We wrote on it:

STOP! LOOK! INJUSTICE

We want Chanal in prison until proven innocent of Trevor O'Keeffe's murder.

Your signature will help get justice for my son.

Please Sign.

Dominique translated it into French for us.

A journalist from the newspaper came with us to document our petition in France. He was young and suffered with asthma so myself and Noeleen felt inclined to mother him a little bit as we went along. We took our homemade placards into the centre of Amiens where the court would be sitting for the appeal. We stopped people and asked them to sign our petition, which a lot of them did. We even had American tourists who stopped to talk with us and who had heard of Chanal. They signed our petition. Then we moved to Chalons-en-Champagne, (formerly Chalons-sur-Marne), positioned ourselves in the local shopping centre and stopped people there to ask them to sign. We went there because it was the nearest town to the army base at Mourmelon, where Chanal had been stationed until 1986. We did it deliberately. It was cheeky of us as most of the people using the centre were soldiers who would most certainly have heard of Chanal. As some of them signed our petition, the centre's security people arrived and practically ran us out of the place, literally marching us out of the shopping mall. We felt like outlaws. It was quite exciting. I really felt we were doing something worthwhile. There we were, two nice, well-dressed ladies approaching middle age, setting up our illegal stall for signatures, then being marched out of town. Mind you, we didn't put up a fight. We didn't want to risk arrest and so damage Trevor's case in any way, so we left and went home to Dublin.

In the end, between our campaign at home and in France, we got thousands of signatures. We felt bold and confident of getting Chanal back behind bars. We just needed the justice system to feel the same.

I put in a request to see the French Minister for Justice, the newly appointed Jacques Toubon, who had only taken office in May 1995 after the election of Jacques Chirac. We had our petition of names that we had collected and we wanted to make sure it got to his door. At the last moment, the minister was unable to meet Noeleen and I because of the fall-out over the French seizure of the Greenpeace vessel, the Rainbow Warrior II. We did, however, see the Executive Chief of Justice Affairs, Olivier de Baynest. I told him how concerned I was for the safety of other young men now that Chanal was released into society. I asked him when was Chanal going to be tried, since he was already charged with Trevor's murder? I knew that, under French law, he could be charged, but the case could not proceed until the investigating magistrate had sufficient evidence to pass on to the State Prosecutor. He told us that the minister could contact the investigating magistrate, but that any decision thereafter would be taken without political reference. Basically, we were being told that the Justice Minister could not and would not be involved. We were on our own, as usual.

We went back to court on 18 July 1995 to seek to have Chanal's bail judgement overturned. We were sure of getting a result in our favour. Surely the authorities would see sense and return this man to jail?

We got off to a good start with an on-form Eric commanding the court with eloquence and conviction. He argued that Chanal and Trevor had shared the same road on 3 August 1987. 'Chanal used to visit this place at Lac Du Der where Trevor's belongings were found,' he said. 'The technique of strangulation was similar to the Hungarian boy,' he continued, referring to the way in which Palazs Falvay had been tied up. Eric argued that Chanal had lied about his schedule between 3 and 10 August. He had said he was going to Verdun but it was now known that he wasn't. He pointed out that the soil found on the spade in Chanal's van was the same as the soil at Trevor's burial place. He concluded with a call for a new analysis of the soil samples.

Buffard, Chanal's lawyer, then put up his arguments and brought in a doctor to testify that the ropes and chains found in Chanal's van could not have been used to strangle Trevor. He said he had proved this by trying to strangle himself from behind to see the marks they left. I couldn't believe this nonsense; if it weren't so serious it would have been laughable.

Chanal then gave his own account as to why he had so many underpants in his van. He said he needed different types for different activities. So, for example, if he were running, he'd wear a small pair; if he were jumping out of an aeroplane, he would need a large pair. If he were doing another activity, he would wear a different pair. This was the reason he gave for having so many different sizes in his possession, even though there were some that, no matter what, would never have fitted him at all. What surprised us even more than this, frankly ludicrous, excuse was that he was actually issued with regulation underpants by the army. None of these other underpants were the plain white army issue. In relation to the underpants that I knew belonged to Trevor, Chanal said he had bought them by mail order from Marks and Spencer in Paris.

Chanal was deemed to be '*mis en examen*' or 'under investigation' in relation to Trevor's case, but in the meantime he would remain free. More evidence would be needed to convict him in a court. The judge ordered another investigation of the soil samples and ordered that a trial should take place not later than a year from that date. In reality, it was to be almost another six years before we got a trial, and in the meantime Chanal was off, scot-free to stroll the streets of his town and drive further afield in his car. It was a travesty.

The following week, unable to think of anything else to do, I wrote to Marks and Spencer to find out if Chanal could have bought underwear from them by mail order, as he had attested. I discovered that this was not possible for two reasons: firstly they didn't operate a mail order catalogue, and the company had no outlet in Paris at the time Chanal said he ordered underwear from them. I sent on my findings to Eric. But it was too little too late.

Eric was angry after the judgement. He made a stinging complaint to Judge Marien about his conduct. Subsequently he called me with some news: 'Judge Marien is going, transferred to a juvenile court in Paris.' There was to be a new judge appointed. He could hear me smiling down the telephone. 'Thank you, Eric,' I said. All was not lost.

Eric also insisted that Trevor's case would be stronger and have more clout if we teamed up with the families of 'The Disappeared'. Having Trevor's case combined with theirs would also strengthened the families' position because Trevor's was the only body that had been found intact and where the autopsy revealed how he died and could be linked to Chanal. I agreed to whatever he thought best. There was no way I was going to argue with him. He could have asked me to go to the moon and I wouldn't have hesitated.

Judge Pascal Chapart took over the case in 1996. He was the seventh Judge to handle Trevor's case. He was based in Chalons-en-Champagne, and he had only just got his feet in under the table when Noeleen and myself went off to interview him as to his intentions for the case.

On a chilly January morning we were shown into the judge's chambers and what I can only describe as a timid young fellow got up off his chair to welcome us. 'He's far too young to be taking on a case like this,' I whispered to Noeleen. He may have been older, but to me he looked barely thirty. There's no way he's going to be able to handle this, I thought.

Still, he got down to business straight away and we liked his style. Judge Chapart told us he had ruled that all the families of 'The Disappeared', as well as our family, should provide swabs so that they could be DNA tested against those taken from Pierre Chanal's van. This was an historic breakthrough for all of us. He would be in touch as to when it would happen. We left his office relieved, excited and hopeful that, at last, things were moving in our direction. Chanal's days of freedom, I thought, were numbered.

We had an opportunity now with a new magistrate to build and present our case, to get Chanal back into court and a trial under-way. However, things weren't moving nearly fast enough for me and I couldn't wait for Eric to come back to me regarding official responses. I had to move things along myself, with Noeleen's help. I called Eric's office every week, every Friday, without fail. If I didn't get through on the Friday, nothing would stop me calling on Monday, Tuesday, and Wednesday until I did get through. I would call at 6pm Irish time, both because it was cheaper and I knew that his office would still be open, or just about. There was generally someone who could speak English to take the call. If I didn't get the right person in Eric's office, I wouldn't spend time or money trying to make myself understood. I would simply hang up and try again later. There were days when I could have called five times or more. One day, years down the line, I said to Eric that I had called Cherifa, who became our second lawyer on the case and who worked with Eric. 'Good,' said, Eric, 'and you keep ringing Cherifa from now on …' I think he was glad to be able to spread the burden!

I got in touch with the Justice Ministry to arrange another meeting with the French Justice Minster, Jacques Toubon. I wanted to ask him how soon we would be having a trial for Trevor. He had not been able to meet me in July the year before so I hoped he might be free this time. I went through Foreign Affairs in Ireland, and then Paris, to set up the appointment with Elizabeth McCullough who had been most helpful to us. I made all the arrangements by phone and we were booked in on a particular day and time in the first week of February to see the Minister.

Noeleen and I booked a flight for early on the day itself. We gave ourselves loads of time to get to the Palais de Justice in Paris, a fabulous, big building right in the centre of the city. We were glad to be finally meeting someone so high in authority and had worked out in advance all that we needed to say to the Minister. We got there, announced who we were and the official at the door asked us to wait. He came back some minutes later. 'You can't go in,' he said 'you don't have an appointment at this time.' Somewhere along the way the day and time had been changed without us knowing about it. Our meeting didn't happen. Now what would we do? We had to leave Paris and book ourselves on a flight home later that day. What a waste.

Once home, I got onto Foreign Affairs and made another appointment for a week later. This time, I insisted that they write and confirm the date.

A week later, on 14 February, Noeleen and I boarded an early flight from Dublin to Paris. It might have been St Valentine's Day and we were off to the city of love, but there would be little romance in what lay ahead for us. I had received confirmation of our appointment with the Minister by post during the week and had even remembered to bring it with me. Nothing could go wrong this time. We arrived on time and were met at the airport by Elizabeth McCullough who took us to the Minister's office in the Palais de Justice. Two officials, carrying a huge file, bustled into the room. One of the men introduced himself as the Minister's First Secretary. 'The Minister is not available,' he said curtly, 'I shall conduct your meeting.' We would have preferred to see the Minister but the First Secretary was better than nothing. Noeleen and I got out our notebooks and conducted our meeting as per our usual manner. I asked the questions and Noeleen took down the answers. I asked what was happening with Trevor's case, what were the police doing, what was the system doing, what had been done, how was the case moving through the system, what had happened to the missing evidence in the case?

The First Secretary opened the huge file. I could see the name on it. It said Chanal. Within the file were a number of smaller files. We assumed these to be those on the missing young conscripts. There was also a file marked 'Trevor O'Keeffe'. The First Secretary took it out and opened it at a page on which we could clearly see Trevor's name. It was an odd mixture of surprise and comfort that such a file existed and that the Minister should have it. The First Secretary apologised for the bad policing that had taken place in the investigation and that they were not proud of what had happened. I was happy to hear this but not what followed. The First Secretary stated quite baldly that Trevor's case was not a case for the State and that we should go home. I stared at the file and thought, if this was none of the Ministry's business, why does this man have Chanal's file, into which Trevor's case is linked? Something didn't quite add up. I looked at Noeleen and knew she was thinking the same thing.

I felt like I was being stupid, that I had missed out on some vital way of doing things that would get us better results and answers. I had the feeling that I was being belittled, that I was a burden, or at worst an aggravation, but all I wanted was to know that the people who were supposed to be doing their jobs and finding and trying my son's killer were doing just that. Was I asking for too much?

Our hour was up and the meeting came to an end. Noeleen and I left the Minister's office and Elizabeth went off to hire a car for us. We were going to Chalons-en-Champagne, about two hours' drive east of Paris in the middle of the Champagne region. I found a phone box and called Eric to tell him what we had been up to. He was surprised to hear from us and even more surprised that we had just come from the Palais de Justice. When we told him of our meeting, he confirmed our own unease about the meeting: why couldn't the ministry tell us anything about the case and yet they had Chanal's file and Trevor's file in their possession? 'Look,' he said, 'you have much more important things to be thinking about.'

He was right. We were going to Chalons-en-Champagne for one of the most important breakthroughs in the whole case. At last, new technology could ultimately prove Chanal's role in the murder of Trevor and the disappearances of the young conscripts. Our families' DNA would be the key. This was going to be a first for my family in other ways, too. Judy was now thirty-one, Tootsie was thirty and James was twenty-nine. Ever since Trevor had died, my family had each done their grieving in isolation of one another. We wanted to spare each other from the awful pain we were going through. When we did come together as a family, we would talk about Trevor and how we felt about him and then we would cry, but we didn't articulate the aching hole he had left in our lives.

I deliberately did not tell the rest of the family the horrible details of how Trevor died; I simply couldn't bear to tell them. I never worried about them ever finding out because I had never allowed them to come with me to France. I felt that I had to spare them even more trauma than they had been through already. My kids were already heartbroken and I couldn't fix it. Now, for the first time, they would be joining Noeleen and I at the courthouse for the DNA testing. For the first time also, they would see up close how the case was going and what was involved. I was confident that there would not be any particular in-depth discussions of the details of how Trevor had died, since all the families of 'The Disappeared' would be present. However, my years of deceit, of not telling them the truth about what happened to their little brother – even though I believed it was for their own good – were to come crashing down around me this on day. And I did not see it coming at all.

Noeleen and I got to Chalons-en-Champagne about midnight and fell into warm beds. We were exhausted and we needed to be ready; tomorrow would be a big day. We woke early, had breakfast and walked the town to fill time until our meeting with the investigating magistrate at 1pm. As we walked around the pretty town, we reflected on the case so far.

Before Judge Chapart had taken over the case, the soil samples that had been at the heart of the case against Chanal in relation to Trevor's murder had mysteriously been 'lost' for a number of years. They turned up again when he took over. These samples, from Chanal's van and Trevor's grave, had originally been deemed to be the same, but had been discounted by the investigating magistrate, Judge Marien. The judge had also decided that the numerous hairs found in the van were not suitable for analysis. Noeleen and I had never been convinced of this.

In the meantime, we had tried to do our own research and Noeleen had found out about a system called Polymerase testing which was available in the USA. She asked me to ask Eric Dupond-Moretti about it. I rang Eric's office and spoke to the secretary there and had an awful job explaining what I was on about – pronouncing the word to her, then spelling it out. In the end we found that it wasn't available in Europe.

We were left hanging as regards these crucial pieces of evidence which were discredited, discounted, then lost over the years.

Now, today, we had an opportunity to bring these crucial finds to the forefront of the case. It was like a dream coming true.

Noeleen and I turned up at the Palais de Justice in the town at the appointed time and were surprised to find it shut for lunch until 1.30pm. We went off for a coffee and came back half an hour later. This time our surprise was that we seemed to be the only ones there; we were expecting hordes of people, between the families of 'The Disappeared' and the media. My gang were also nowhere to be seen. We asked the guard stationed at the reception desk for the investigating magistrate. He said he was out. So we waited. After a time, he came out to us and after some discussion back and forth, in bad French and worse English, we all realised we should in fact be somewhere else entirely. We got a police escort to the right location, the police station. By the time we got there the place was swarming with journalists. Judy, Tootsie and James were waiting for us. They looked lost amid the bustle of people. There was no time for any discussion and the kids were totally taken aback by the media scrum. I had become used to it and it had never dawned on me to warn them about it.

We met our journalist friend, Dominique Rizet, who told us that he wasn't allowed inside and had to stay outside with the other reporters. The rest of us walked in with the families of the 'Disappeared'. Eric joined us and we noticed that all the families had brought their lawyers. Eric apologised for the fact that he would have to leave early. I didn't think that would be a problem. As far as I was concerned, the night ahead consisted of giving some samples of our DNA, and maybe hearing an address from the judge before going home. We were directed into a big room – a courtroom with seats and benches facing forward. There were between thirty and forty people there, with two or three policemen stationed about the walls. As we went in, we were brought in turn into a doctor's room and gave blood samples from which they would test the DNA. We then got seats towards the rear of the room, but could plainly see what was going on at the front.

Judge Chapart was addressing the gathering. To his left there was a television; they were obviously going to show us something. We were the only family who did not speak French, and, while we were provided with a policeman who said he could speak English, quite soon it was clear that he couldn't translate for us at all. In fact, he pretended to speak English to us, and as Judge Chapart conducted proceedings at the top of the room, he would whisper to us. To look at us, anyone would think that he was translating what was being said, but we knew he wasn't. It was farcical. So there we were, the five of us, myself, Judy, Tootsie, James and Noeleen, with this crowd of other people who all knew what was happening but we didn't. We couldn't follow any of what the judge was saying, except that he seemed to be telling the families that we should look carefully at what we were about to see in order to try and identify our sons. It was desperately frustrating, but to be honest, after all I had been through previously in terms of mishandling of the case, it was little more than I expected. I think it was much more daunting for my kids. They had no idea what was going on at all.

The lights dimmed and photographs appeared on the television screen in front of us. They showed individuals and groups of people who looked like they were tourists in holiday gear, with cameras around their necks. I didn't recognise anyone in these shots. Then we saw pictures that appeared as though they were shot on cine film; they were taken from the ground, looking up at a helicopter, and could have been army training clips, but didn't seem to feature any soldiers. I had no idea why we were being shown this footage and I'm sure my kids were wondering just what they were doing here, in a courtroom in the middle of France watching some random pictures that seemed to have no relation whatever to the case.

Then, without any warning to us at all, a video started to play on the screen. Initially the pictures showed a parachute jump and shots of green fields and birds. It looked like somebody's personal camcorder recordings. Then, all of a sudden, the scene changed and the screen was filled with the image of a young man, lying down, naked and with his feet chained. His face was not visible. The young man was tied to a makeshift camper bed by a contraption that was made of tubular steel scaffolding. His arms were chained at the wrists to this scaffold. You could hear the chains clanking when he moved. It was shocking.

My kids said, 'Jesus Christ, Mum, what are we watching this for?' It suddenly clicked with me that this was a video of one of the victims who had been abducted by Chanal. Chanal had set up his video recorder and framed the shot deliberately. Next Chanal could be seen with some homemade wooden contraption that induced an orgasm. We saw everything: his genitals as he masturbated. The images continued for a full hour. More young men's bodies, more abuse, more evil. Other photographs followed: still pictures of boys who were tied up. It seemed to me to go on forever. My head was swimming. These were obviously videos found in his premises, his rooms and van.

As I said previously, I had kept from my kids all the details relating to what Chanal had done to his victims. And now they were seeing this. As the video images continued, I grew nauseous, knowing that the full extent of Chanal's degeneracy and what he was capable of doing to his victims, including their brother, would be dawning on them too.

What was the point of showing us this? I thought. Did they think we would recognise one of these young men as Trevor? It seemed grossly unnecessary. My kids were distraught. I was so angry then that they were being made to watch this filth. No matter that it was evidence and that Chanal's horrific behaviour had to be acknowledged so that we could get him to court, it just wasn't right. This was the last thing I wanted my kids to be confronted with. Hadn't they been through enough traumas already? I couldn't even look at them. Inside, I raged about the injustice of it all, my head brimming with the images passing before me. Noeleen sat quietly beside me. She was watching every frame of the video with such intensity. She didn't want to miss a vital clue that would somehow help us with our case. She told me afterwards that she was staring at the pictures to see if there was a little mark here or a little mark there that she could say to me, 'Eroline, do you recognise that, did Trevor have a mark here or a mark there?' She had been amazed at how young and blemish-free each and every one of the young men were, as if Chanal had handpicked them especially for his sinister purposes. How she managed to maintain her composure I do not know. I couldn't. All those images are still in my head, and what makes it much worse is that I have no doubt they are in the nightmares of my children.

When the videos finished, I was surprised to see that I wasn't the only angry parent. The French families were in uproar. I had thought that they might have been prepared for what they were about to see. But this was obviously the first time they had seen such footage too. Judge Chapart, whose idea this had been, was in the courtroom. The families lit on him, yelling and screaming at him, shaking their fists. He, quite literally, ran off. He was only a young fellow and I felt he was going to cry. I would say he really felt quite threatened. The scene was one of pandemonium, families crying and shouting all around us. We didn't stay. The five of us quickly made our escape.

As we emerged from this nightmare, we were beset by flashing cameras. We were mobbed. Photographers even lay on the bonnet of our car to get pictures of us inside. We kept both cars going, all the way to Caroline's house in Chantilly. Once there, all hell broke loose. I felt that my family were going to kill me. All three ganged up on me and we had the mightiest row. 'How could you keep this from us?' they screamed, 'and for so many years?' 'How could you not tell us what really happened to Trevor, what this monster did to him?' Caroline tried to referee, but it was no use. The kids needed to yell and maybe I needed to hear it. Noeleen went off to bed and left us to it.

The next day, James, Tootsie and Judy got the train to London together. The air was thick with recrimination and despair, but we hugged goodbye. Noeleen, Caroline and I went to the airport. Once there, we discovered that Noeleen had left her bag, with her passport, in Chantilly. She and Caroline went back for it and I continued on to Dublin on my own.

A month later I wrote to Judge Chapart with six demands. I asked for a complete synopsis of the investigations carried out by his departments from 3 August 1987 to the present day, 26 March

1997. I asked to review the videos shown to us, saying we had not been informed as to the reason why we were viewing the videos or their importance, due to the interpreter's poor English. I also asked to view any of Chanal's property now in the possession of the police department. Finally I asked for an update on the progress of the DNA testing and if the investigators had ever carried out a 'polymerase chain reaction testing technique'.

I sent the letter to Eric who then put the request to the judge in April. My six queries became two which he could feasibly base on questions of procedure: that the articles confiscated from the camping Volkswagen of Pierre Chanal be shown to me and that we also have a second showing of the videos seized due to the fact we had not understood the implications of the previous showing through inadequate interpretation and explanation.

Eric told me that the judge would have a month in which to answer the request. If he answered in the negative, he would provide a ruling stating the legal reasons for rejection, which must be appealed within ten days of being notified of the ruling. 'If he rejects the request,' Eric wrote, 'we will appeal and the matter will be considered by the Chief Justice of the criminal division of the Court of Appeal, who w ill decide whether or not to refer the question to the Court of Appeal.' Meanwhile he would keep me updated with developments.

On 22 November 1996 Noeleen and I went back to France to see Judge Chapart in his chambers in the Palais de Justice in Chalons. He had something to show us. We were astounded when he produced photographs of Chanal's property from his Volkswagen van. I had been asking to see the contents of Chanal's van and his room for over a decade and here, for the first time, my request was being honoured. Noeleen and I examined every photograph for anything that looked like it might be Trevor's. There were photographs of tools, chains, weights, a gas heater, a cylinder, gloves, including rubber gloves, and a rope. There were other photographs showing a denim jacket, a torn top, and trousers. Unfortunately there was nothing we could identify as belonging to Trevor. What Judge Chapart then told us astonished us even more. He revealed that the property found in Chanal's van was burned by the police after he went to prison and that the army had requested full access to his former living quarters around the same time. They needed the room for someone else. Chanal's sister was invited to the barracks to collect whatever she wanted from his belongings. Whatever she left behind was burned.

I couldn't believe what I was hearing. I was horrified. It took a moment or two for me to regain composure. I took a deep breath before replying to this astounding news.

'How,' I asked, 'in an ongoing murder inquiry, as Trevor's case is, could the main suspect's room and possessions – all potential and possibly crucial evidence – be destroyed?' I waited for a reply. None came. I asked another question.

'How come the police had not seized all this property earlier?'

The judge simply stuck to his line about the army needing to take the room back. He didn't engage at all in my questioning.

There was more for Judge Chapart to tell us. We listened in rapt silence. When Judge Chapart took over the case he ordered a new search of Chanal's van that turned up 600 hairs from the mattress Chanal had kept in back of the van. This evidence included a hundred new hairs that had not been documented before. This was a substantial increase in the original number reportedly found, which was 400. However there was a downside to the whole process. He explained that it would take four months to analyse one hair. I finally broke our silence and spluttered, 'does this mean 600 hairs multiplied by four months, because if that's the case, by the time the results come through, we'll all be dead!'

'Yes,' he replied, 'it is a very long time!'

Loïc Le Ribault had done the site testing on Chanal's shovel in 1988. He was the first scientist who had access to Chanal's van. He had discovered that the particles found on Chanal's shovel could be matched perfectly with the soil in which Trevor had been buried.

We had been told the original soil samples had been mislaid and no more analysis could be carried out on them. But Judge Chapart found that there was indeed sufficient soil available to do new tests. The results were the same as before: soil on Chanal's shovel matched soil found where Trevor was buried. Nothing had changed in all the intervening years.

Noeleen and I returned home. I felt we were treading water, waiting, waiting for something to happen. The frustration was building. I called Eric's office every week and no matter who answered, they had all learnt to say 'No news, Eroline' in English. Throughout 1997, little happened in our particular case but French President Chirac had announced a major overhaul of the justice system. On television he said, 'Justice does not respond to the needs of the French. Many of you find it too slow, sometimes too expensive and difficult to understand.' I agreed wholeheartedly, and for us foreigners, these problems were a hundred times worse. I sought out other cases that bore a similarity to Trevor's, including that of English student teacher Joanna Parrish who had been found strangled on a riverbank in the picturesque town of Auxerre in central France in 1990. Her parents had suffered a similar fate to me: lacklustre police investigation, silence from the magistrate and no discernable movement on the case for over six years. Yet they too had continued to go to Auxerre and find out for themselves what they could to bring the perpetrator to trial. Though I never got in touch with the family directly, I looked for and kept newspaper cuttings relating to the case. I felt isolated, that our case wasn't being dealt with properly and we were running out of people to turn to for help.

Lara Marlowe, the Paris-based *Irish Times* journalist, wrote a searing piece where she highlighted that of the 1500 people who were murdered in France each year, only 40% of murder cases actually led to a conviction. She went on to say that of the twenty-four English people who had been murdered over the previous twenty years, only four of the cases led to convictions. The odds of us ever getting Chanal to trial looked slim.

In December 1998, and as if conjured out of thin air, Loïc Le Ribault, the scientist who had carried out the original soil sample analysis, sought us out and asked for a meeting. The encounter was bizarre, although it's only when I look back on it now that the secret meetings and remote assignations look odd. At the time, Noeleen and I would have gone anywhere at any time of the day or night to talk to anyone who had something new to say about Trevor's case. We were at the end of our tether. We believed that the whole affair with Chanal stank of military collusion and protectionism. We had been promised our day in court over a year before and nothing, absolutely nothing was happening as Chanal roamed free. Of course we could have done with being a little more discerning in whom we took up with as newfound friends, but at the time, we never gave it another thought.

It began when Harry Magee, a journalist with the *Sunday Tribune*, contacted me and said, 'We have someone here who has all the information that links Chanal to Trevor's murder and he wants to meet you.' I knew exactly who he was talking about and I was keen to meet him. I held my composure and said, 'OK, where is he and when does he want to meet?' Harry gave me the address of a hotel in Pontoon, County Mayo and Noeleen and I went off in her car to meet the secretive stranger. Loïc Le Ribault introduced himself in a cloud of strong French cigarette smoke. He was in his early fifties, refined and dressed impeccably but incongruously in an off-season navy blue blazer and grey slacks. While we had not met him before, we had read that he was a flamboyant and publicity-hungry scientist. It was he who was responsible for the original soil sample analysis on Chanal's spade and the soil taken from where Trevor had been buried. He had been contracted to make the analysis based on his own original technique. The authorities stopped using his technique and eventually his laboratory had to close. However he had kept the original sample analysis document, as well as a twenty-five page dossier on Chanal, and now he wanted us to have it. He told us to keep it safe, to lock it away in a bank or somewhere like that. He said it revealed that Chanal was not only the murderer of Trevor but was, in fact, a serial killer and responsible for multiple deaths. He told us not to keep the document in my house, that Noeleen and I could be killed for it because it incriminated Chanal in Trevor's murder. He told us he was actually on the run; people were after him because of the file. He also said that there was a six-hour videotape of the forensic search of Chanal's van that had never been seen by the families.

We didn't question anything he told us. I was only too ready to accept the document and try to use it to get us to trial more speedily. It was all I thought about. Even Noeleen, who was the voice of reason on all other matters, became embroiled in the saga when she actually allowed him to stay as a lodger in her house for a couple of months in Celbridge. We believed him; after all, Judge Chapart was preparing to accept his soil sample analysis as evidence against Chanal. I sent the file to Eric. 'Keep away from this man,' he said, 'There is nothing in this file I don't already know about.' He told me that an allegation had been made that Loïc had stolen the file and that he was wanted in France, which would have explained his being 'on the run'.

Deep down, Noeleen and I did acknowledge that the man might also be the greatest 'chancer' we'd ever met, but we generally kept these thoughts to ourselves. Noeleen had a Garda friend who checked out that Loïc was indeed wanted for arrest in France. We were so desperate to have something to move the case on and our paranoia about the French authorities was so great that no matter where the information came from, we were happy to get it, so we simply ignored the fact that police in France wanted Loïc.

On 20 January 1999, Noeleen phoned me. I could hear the barely contained excitement in her voice, 'There is new evidence.

They're talking about Chanal being charged. It's been on the news already. Caroline has just been watching it on French television.' We believed it would only be a matter of time now before Chanal was arrested and a trial called. At last, the wheels of French justice were turning. But in the meantime there were more worrying problems closer to home, in Mayo in fact.

That night Noeleen got an urgent call from Loïc. He had stayed in her house in Celbridge for eight weeks from the beginning of December, and had returned to Mayo only days before, when a friend of his gave him a house to stay in. Noeleen went off into the night in search of the house, which was up in the mountains beyond Pontoon, County Mayo. The road was so remote that you would hardly know it existed at all. Noeleen drove for five hours in the middle of the night through snow to the house. God only knows how she found it. Loïc was in a terrible state. His male assistant, Luke, who was HIV positive, was close to death.

Without asking one question about him, Noeleen put the man in her car and drove back home at twenty-seven miles an hour in the falling snow. She called a doctor acquaintance. The doctor examined him. 'Noeleen, get rid of this man at once,' he said. 'He's dying. What will you do if he dies on your floor? Do you even know his second name?' Noeleen didn't know his surname. But she was a doctor of Chinese medicine and kept the man for a number of weeks and, amazingly, nursed him back to health. As far as we know, he's still alive and well today. We still keep in contact with Loïc and now and again see him when he comes to Ireland. He offered himself as a witness if and when we ever got to trial and would have taken part via satellite if he couldn't return to France without some guarantee that he wouldn't be arrested there.

Noeleen and I weren't the only people so frustrated with the justice system we would resort to desperate measures. One of the 'Disappeared' families had taken the French government to the European Court of Human Rights. The French government was found guilty of violating Article 6 of the European Declaration on Human Rights, which ensures the right to justice within a reasonable amount of time. Their case had taken seven and a half years to reach court. Trevor's case was now twelve years old.

In October 1999, Noeleen and I were invited onto a television programme about Chanal to be broadcast on the French TV2 channel. Stefan Breitmer, a journalist whom we knew, called Noeleen to organise the filming and passed on some important new information that we hadn't been aware of. He said that the DNA results were coming through, presenting new evidence that confirmed that Trevor had been in Chanal's van and also that Patrick Gache and Patrice Denis had also been in the van. The completed DNA tests confirmed that some of the 400 hair fragments found in Chanal's van belonged to Trevor, Patrick Gache and Patrice Denis. Further forensic tests reconfirmed that soil in Chanal's van was identical to that found in Trevor's shallow grave, 100km from the military base where Chanal was posted.

André Buffard, Chanal's lawyer, had immediately demanded that all the tests be re-done. This sounded like a stalling tactic to me, after all, DNA testing has been around for a long time and is a very accurate science. Judge Chapart rejected Buffard's request in every case except one – Trevor's. The test was re-done in a laboratory in Strasbourg. Some months later the result came back, it was the same result.

Stefan Breitmer had been following Chanal's movements and said that the police had stepped up surveillance on him at his home near Lyons, making him report daily to them and barring him from driving. During the appeals, Eric had argued that there were striking similarities between the Falvay case and Trevor's. Stefan told us that Chanal's lawyer was now arging that Chanal had served his time in prison for that particular crime and there was no reason why the case should be re-investigated and evidence used in relation to another case. 'But most importantly of all,' he warned us, 'the judge will need to move fast because we know that Chanal may commit suicide.' I believed this to be true because Chanal had been quoted in the press as saying he would rather die than go back to prison, and I reckoned he meant it.

However, Stefan was confident: 'We know the judge will charge Chanal,' he said, 'in two weeks, three at the most, no more than that.'

CHAPTER 10

Justice at Last?

A year later, in September 2000, Chanal was charged with eight murders, seven of them being the 'Disappeared' young men and the eighth was Trevor. However, Chanal fought back with everything he and his lawyer had and successfully appealed the number of charges against him. One by one, the charges were reduced. At this rate, we could find ourselves with no case at all to be answered. In the intervening time, Noeleen and I did interviews, talking to journalists in Ireland and France, to keep the case in the public arena. I was still not allowed to mention Chanal by name but it was second nature by then. We travelled to France perhaps a half dozen times. I continued to make my weekly phone calls to Eric as well as to our new lawyer, Eric's law partner, Cherifa Benmouffok.

All in all, the case was at least moving in the right direction and we were hopeful that a trial would be just around the corner. Nothing could have prepared us for the awful tragedy that was about to befall us.

In November, 2000, Caroline, Noeleen's beautiful daughter and my niece, was found dead in her home in France in what we later discovered were highly suspicious circumstances. Caroline, slim, pretty, yet as resolute as Noeleen and I, had been our eyes and ears in France since the beginning. She was the person to whom we turned to lead us through the language problems; she was the one person who was always ready with her car and her home whenever we needed them; the one who, through all these years, helped steady our nerves before a meeting with the authorities and held our hands afterwards as we ranted against the inadequacies of the system. And now she was gone, taken from us. She was barely into her thirties.

She was a wonderful young woman who was fit and healthy, a female jockey in a man's world. The police said she had committed suicide but that did not ring true to anyone who knew and loved her. The police claimed that she had killed herself by taking poison, but they failed to carry out an investigation. As in Trevor's case, bad policing was more than evident from the outset. Caroline's house had been emptied and cleaned within hours of her having been found dead. We don't know by whom. No autopsy was carried out. When Noeleen asked for an autopsy, the police said there was no need for an autopsy, and that one was not available in France. Noeleen then said she was taking her daughter home to her own family.

For ten months after Caroline died, Noeleen couldn't do much beyond getting up in the morning, eating and going to bed. She was deeply disturbed by Caroline's death. It was an enormous shock. I knew how she felt and I left her alone until she needed me.

When she did eventually decide to start asking questions, she realised that nothing had been done in the case. There had been no autopsy and so the police had not followed up evidence. Noeleen had brought Caroline's body home and arranged to have an autopsy carried out in Ireland by pathologist Dr Marie Cassidy. The results came through after five months. What they revealed was that there was no poison in Caroline's system. She was found to have been beaten for three days before she died. There were over forty bruises on her body, with the bruises on her lower legs attributable to someone repeatedly dropping a heavy object on them. She also had two knife slashes across her chest. Caroline had not committed suicide.

Dr Cassidy advised Noeleen to get herself a lawyer because she believed Caroline's death was suspect.

It would take Noeleen a further ten months to get an investigating magistrate to be appointed to Caroline's case. She has been pursuing the matter since, and, so far, nothing has been done.

In March 2001, Caroline was cremated and part of her ashes were buried in Mount Jerome cemetery in Harold's Cross in Dublin; then we went to France to scatter the remainder of the ashes on the racecourse at Chantilly as a final memorial to her. Noeleen and I went on to Paris, where we separated to go to our respective legal advisors. Noeleen had her first meeting with a lawyer she had engaged in Paris, while I went to Lille to see Eric.

The terrible irony of our double tragedy was not lost on us. Just as we felt we were coming to the end of one ordeal, another had started. I don't know how Noeleen kept going and was still there for me; she never once buckled under it all. I was in awe of her.

At this point I worked out how much I'd spent so far on Trevor's case. It was tens of thousands of pounds in flights, accommodation and legal fees during over thirty visits to France over a fourteen-year period. I checked my dwindling bank balance and asked myself if I would have to continue my campaign for another fourteen years?

On 10 August 2001, just after the fourteenth anniversary of Trevor's death, and after many cross-examinations, Judge Chapart finally charged Pierre Chanal with the abductions and murders of Patrice Denis, Patrick Gache and Trevor O'Keeffe.

These were the only three cases that, using the new DNA analysis, could be positively identified as being connected to Chanal. Trevor's case was deemed the strongest because there was a body and an autopsy to draw on. The body of Olivier Donner, although recovered, had been too decomposed to yield any useful results. This meant that in his case and in the cases of the other boys, Patrick Dubois, Serge Havet, Manuel Carvalho and Pascal Sergent, the judge had to dismiss the cases as there was not enough evidence to charge Chanal with their disappearances and murders. It was a devastating blow for the families after so many years of heartache, questioning and campaigning. I realised then how much hope was riding on the success of our three cases. If Chanal could be convicted, it might offer the opportunity for the other cases to be reopened and examined further. We all believed, without any doubt, that Chanal had murdered our sons, that he was a serial killer and we all believed that sooner or later he would be proven guilty.

The case went to the Chief Prosecutor, who viewed the file, then set the date and court for the trial. It was only then it started to sink in: we were finally getting a trial. My first reaction was disbelief that it was happening at last and that Chanal was, after so many years as prime suspect, facing trial for what he had done. There was an unreality in the period following Chanal's arrest. It was too good to be true. Noeleen and I couldn't believe our luck; we were on the lookout for the flaws in our good fortune.

We turned our attention to Chanal. Now that a trial had actually been ordered, we believed that Chanal could no longer be protected. We were convinced that the evidence was so strong that he would be convicted. And we believed Chanal felt this way too.

I spent the remainder of 2001 and into 2002 in a state of nervous expectation, waiting for word of the trial, waiting for word of another suicide attempt by Chanal. In May 2002, Eric wrote to me, exasperated. He said he wanted me to take a case against the French State for the shortcomings in its justice system. He had written to the Minister for Justice requesting an inquiry into the delays in the case. Regarding the lawsuit, Eric said that he would demand €150,000 in damages for 'grievous error'. But the money wasn't important to me. All I wanted was to get Chanal into that courtroom, but if it took a lawsuit to get the French State to acknowledge that it had delayed, obfuscated and generally dragged its heels in the case to have justice done for my son, then so be it. I filed the lawsuit, and, as usual, waited.

In the meantime I kept up the pressure on Chanal as best I could. By 2003, the evidence was stacked as high as it could be against him, and though we still didn't have a trial date, I believed he knew what he stood to lose if he was sent back to jail.

He had said many times that he did not want and would not go back to jail. After all, here was a man devoted to the outdoor life, an obsessive skydiver who loved to be soaring through the skies, free as a bird. He would do anything he could to get out of incarceration and he had the singular will and specialist commando training to make sure he could do a competent job on himself, so long as he had the resources. We felt the authorities would need to be extra vigilant with Chanal. They would need to be watching him constantly. In his hands, the most innocent piece of equipment could be an instrument of self-harm and death. He had already used an ordinary razor to cut his wrists in order to get out of the first appeal, back in 1994. He had spent over a decade as the prime suspect; how long could his luck last? In interviews with the judge, he called Noeleen and I his 'persecutors' and I quite liked that. It meant he was afraid of us and that was good.

I got to meet the Chief Prosecutor, Yves Charpenel, myself. The first thing I noticed about him was that he spoke excellent English and I was pleasantly surprised. After all these years I felt I could understand people much better than when I had started out but I always felt much more relieved if we met someone who would speak to us in English.

The second thing I noticed was how genuinely reassuring he was. Slim-built and refined, he told me what his role was: to view the file and see fit for it to go to court, then set the date and court and put the judges in place. He said I could ring him anytime to ask any question about the case and how it would be conducted. I was stunned by his attitude; I certainly had not encountered this welcoming, open style before. Needless to say, I did ring him, and on numerous occasions, too. Well, he had said I could! I called him to ask when was the trial going to happen, and how soon would we be going to court? There had been a few trials in the past involving serial killers and they generally dragged on because of the collation of evidence from so many sources, but Chanal's trial had been through so many false starts and such delays, especially in the first decade. It seemed hard to believe that a trial would ever happen, never mind anytime soon. Eventually though, my phone calls to the Chief Prosecutor paid off and I got my answer.

Around the beginning of April, I received some important official documents. The trial would take place at the Court of Assizes at Reims on 12 May. But we had a problem. This was also the date that my daughter, Judy, was getting married in the Dominican Republic.

What would I do? Even though we all knew the trial would be coming up, we did not have an exact date and so Judy, like any sane person would, had gone ahead and made her wedding arrangements. Noeleen and I had for so many years put whatever we needed to on hold, often permanently; an operation for me, a hip replacement for Noeleen, and now, saddest of all, my own daughter's wedding.

So while my daughter, her fiancé and the rest of my family would be celebrating her special day in the Dominican Republic, Noeleen and I would be sitting in court in Reims. Though heartbroken that I wouldn't be with her, I couldn't actually see any other way around it. I simply had to go to court.

For the first time we had lots of offers of translators, both from our own Department of Foreign Affairs and from Judge Chapart in France. After sixteen years of not having a translator with us in court, it felt odd. Late though it was in proceedings, we accepted a translator from Yves Charpenel, the Chief Prosecutor, who, I have to say, supplied me with a brilliant translator. Before getting to court, she had phoned to ask all about the case so she would be properly prepared. I was very much looking forward to hearing every word that was going to be said. Things were looking hopeful.

As the trial date approached, Noeleen and I were on our way home from a meeting with the Chief Prosecutor one day. We were in Reims railway station. I was minding the bags while Noeleen went off to get the tickets. At the desk she asked the clerk what was the time of the next train. She misheard the answer and thought the train was leaving immediately so was just darting off to collect me and the luggage when a lady in the queue called out, in perfect English, 'You're all right, the train is not due for another twenty minutes.' Noeleen stopped to thank the woman and off we went to the train. At the barrier, our tickets got stuck and the same woman came to our rescue again and told us to try another machine. She was very friendly. 'Where are you both from?' she asked. 'We're from Dublin.' I looked at Noeleen who then said quickly, 'Well, she's from Kildare, I'm from Dublin.' 'So am I,' said the woman, 'and what are you doing here?' Now, we had been going to France for sixteen years and in all that time we had never encouraged nor engaged in conversation with anyone outside of Trevor's case. We had always kept our heads down and got on with things. Invariably someone somewhere would ask were we on holiday and we always, quite firmly, said 'no, we were on business' and left it at that. But for some reason, which neither Noeleen nor myself could put a finger on, we looked at each other and we told her exactly why we were there. To our surprise, she knew all about Trevor's case and revealed that she had been following it over the years. We got on the train with her but she was only travelling a short distance, a few stops along the line. Before she got off, we told her that the trial would be coming up in May. 'My husband and I have accommodation here,' she said. 'It was our home but we've just moved to a new place in Brittany and I'm almost sure I could give it to you, but I would like to discuss it with my husband first.' We exchanged contact details and said goodbye as she got off at her stop. True to her word, the woman did discuss the idea with her husband and later, back in Ireland, Noeleen and I met the two of them in Dublin. As it turned out, the woman, Pearl, had gone to France as an au pair and met her husband-to-be, Michel, who was in the army. Both knew all about Trevor's case. They actually gave us their home, within walking distance of the court in Reims, for the duration of the trial. We couldn't believe it and were deeply moved by such generosity and trust.

When the time came for the trial, we went to France and the couple had arranged for their neighbours to meet us off the train. It was their home, with all their personal possessions around the place. We couldn't believe this had happened from a chance meeting in a railway station. We felt it might be yet another good omen.

Two days before he was to appear in court, Chanal tried to commit suicide. We had expected it, yet when we heard, it still came as a shock. Was this the end of our run of good luck?

Chanal had taken an overdose and then, according to the version we heard, had gone to a small airfield and lay down on the runway, where he was later found. When Noeleen heard this, she said to me, 'did he hope he was going to be run over by a plane, lying there?' We thought it was laughable and ridiculous but we knew better than to underestimate Chanal's aversion to standing trial. In a letter addressed to the court prior to his suicide attempt, Chanal had still protested his innocence, saying that he 'refused to be judged for something that he hadn't done.' He would not be presenting himself at the Court of Assizes on 13 May and said that he had, therefore, 'taken the decision to put an end to my life and to this calvary which has gone on for too long.' He had also written 'final' letters to his family, so he had been quite serious about it. He finished his letter to his sister by saying, 'I accuse all the false witnesses ... and their calumnious declarations, why did they do this? To all my family, my friends, my accusers, I claim my innocence one last time.' It was clear that Chanal would most definitely try to commit suicide again and, who knows, he might be successful and the trial would collapse. We had no time to lose. We had to keep going, no matter what.

Each day, we went to court expectantly, waiting for news about Chanal. It was ironic that we were hoping the murderer of our sons would get better. But we only had one focus in mind: to get Chanal to trial and get a conviction.

The waiting was excruciating. Noeleen and I reverted to our usual way of passing the time and tramped the streets of Reims. We were literally pacing the streets. For a change we'd get the train into Paris and wander the streets there.

One day we called to the cathedral in Reims where Mass was being said and joined in the congregation. We were there to kill time more than in any great show of devotion, but it was as comforting a place to be as any. Afterwards, we lit candles for Chanal, praying that he would live long enough so that he could stand trial. We were so close to hearing the answers, so close to hearing all the evidence in one place once and for all; we were convinced we were within a hair's breadth of a conviction.

We stayed on in the church as a wedding party appeared. They looked lovely and bright and cheerful in the May sunshine. I thought about my own daughter's big day on the other side of the world. I was in no mood to move on and soon another wedding party arrived, then another. By the time the day was over, Noeleen and I had watched five weddings come and go to the cathedral. Each one made me sadder than the last.

In the evenings, we'd try and divert ourselves from the trial and Chanal. One night we even went to the Folies Bergères in the centre of Paris. It was a welcome relief to pretend to be a tourist.

Another day we were walking through the colourful Pigalle district, with all its exotic shops and even more exotic clientele on show, when we spotted an unlikely traditional bed linen shop. We each bought an eiderdown and pillowcase set packed into specially constructed suitcases which we dragged around Paris after us for days! I think two of our daughters were the lucky recipients once we'd hauled them home.

By 19 May, the court finally decided to postpone the trial due to Chanal's ill health. A new trial date was set, this time for 14 October 2003. There was nothing else we could do but pack up our bags and go home. We would come back in October.

Meanwhile, on a beautiful Caribbean beach, my daughter and the rest of my family had celebrated her wedding. Not only had I missed it, but there hadn't even been a trial to make the sacrifice worthwhile.

Chanal was transferred to the psychiatric hospital in Villejuif in Val-De-Marne, but was well enough to leave by the end of June.

He was still kept under observation for his own safety. Back home in Naas, I kept up my own surveillance of him through phone calls to France.

In July, Chanal began a hunger strike in Fresnes, a jail near Paris. He was put into isolation so his condition could be monitored. Every day I woke up, thinking, will he die today? I hope he doesn't. Please God, let him live until October.

I would then call Dominique or Eric or Foreign Affairs or the Chief Prosecutor, and sometimes all of them, one after the other, to check that Chanal was still alive.

Eric told me that I would be called to give my evidence on the second day of the trial. As much as the prospect of going up on the stand terrified me, I was actually looking forward to my day in court. I prepared as much as I could. I remembered everything about the night I got the phone call from Tootsie and the weeks, months and years afterwards when we tried to find out who had murdered my son. Eric said he would take me through it before the trial began but it was all in my head anyway, had never gone away.

The strain of waiting and watching for news of Chanal's fluctuating health was enormous. As October approached, we made our plans. My three eldest, Judy, James and Tootsie, decided that they wanted to come to the trial. It would be only their second time accompanying me. I hoped to God that it wouldn't be as bad as the first time when they had been made to watch that horrific videotape of Chanal abusing a host of young men. Even though my kids were in their thirties, they were still my babies, they still needed protection as far as I was concerned, and I didn't care how many times they told me they could look after themselves.

By October, Chanal was under constant supervision and was not well enough to attend the trial. The whole case could collapse right before our eyes. It looked like Chanal might be winning after all.

Our hopes dulled, the kids and I went off to Reims for preliminary court hearings. Just before the trial was due to begin in earnest, Eric went into court and made a startling request. He argued that the trial should continue without Chanal. This was unheard of in French law. There were excited gasps around the room. I looked to the judges' bench; would they agree to such a controversial request? Chanal's lawyer went ballistic, screaming and roaring that his client was not being given a rightful hearing. The courtroom of victims' families however murmured its own hopeful verdict. The judges excused themselves and went off to a side chamber to deliberate while we all waited anxiously, checking our watches. It was quite literally turning into a race against time, a race to get the evidence to trial before Chanal could fulfil his death wish and stop it. The judges returned sombrely to the courtroom to give their decision. Their faces gave nothing away. They took their seats and then one prepared to speak. No one even dared cough lest they miss the ruling. The judge spoke slowly and deliberately. Our interpreter followed suit, translating word for word. For the first time in my long French court history, I missed not one word of what was being said. I was amazed by what I heard. The trial would continue without Chanal. A communal sigh of relief echoed around the courtroom. That's one for us, Trevor, I whispered quietly. To the side of the court was an empty chair. It was Chanal's. It was a visceral reminder of the tenuous line between trial and collapse. It was hard to look anywhere else.

We approached every hour uncertainly, expecting the word to come that Chanal had finally succeeded in killing himself. I suspect even Chanal himself would have been amazed that the trial was going ahead without him. He would not have been prepared for that outcome at all and I'm sure it only quickened his resolve to suicide.

On the day of the trial, 14 October 2003, Noeleen, myself and my three kids got to the court in Reims at 8.30 in the morning. We met first with Nicole, our interpreter. Eric joined us later. The media were out in force, with cameras everywhere. But for Noeleen and I the most welcome sight was that of all the families of 'The Disappeared' who had come to the trial, even though most of them would not be getting justice for their own sons on this occasion. Some hoped that our three cases would be the start of something. If Chanal were found guilty, then their cases might be looked at again, and maybe sometime down the road, Chanal would stand trial for the abduction and murder of their sons. I hoped that this trial would give them hope, a hope for justice for their boys.

The judges arrived and solemnly took their seats on the bench. There were five of them. The room was so much bigger than the courts I had been used to for the appeals back in 1995. It was old and there were rows of seats allocated to the families, to witnesses and to lawyers. The jury arrived and were sworn in. The trial would go on all day as there was a lot to get through. It was scheduled to sit for three weeks. It was busy and businesslike. The State would start by calling its witnesses. Buffard was there for Chanal and the plan was that as the days progressed and he was deemed fit enough, he could be brought down to the trial in a wheelchair. For today, however, he would remain in his hospital bed. Maybe we would see him tomorrow. Eric and Cherifa were there for me, along with the other families and their lawyers. It was a historic day. After so many years of delays, I couldn't quite believe it was all happening. And all happening today. It felt that it was nothing short of a miracle. I wanted to pinch myself to make sure it was actually real and I wasn't fantasising.

Noeleen and I watched as a thin, gaunt figure, dressed head to foot in black combat-style clothes, ducked into the courtroom, pulling a huge scarf around its face so as not to be seen. The figure sat opposite us. We had no idea who the person was, male or female. Until they were called for the defence, that is.

Simone, Chanal's sister unwrapped her scarf to reveal part of her face as she took the stand. She spoke very quietly and was asked several times to speak up. Our translator also strained to hear what she was saying. I not only strained to hear her but also had to strain to hear our interpreter who could only whisper while court was going on. It was an intense experience, to say the least.

Chanal's sister spoke for an hour, talking about how wonderful her brother was as a brother, son, and uncle. A judge stopped her at one point and asked, 'why, if Chanal was such a good son, did he not contact his mother for seven years?' Later, when she spoke about Chanal and his father, he asked why had Chanal not attended his father's funeral? This was a great start to the day and the trial. Already Chanal was looking discredited. I wished that he were here so that I could watch his discomfort.

There then followed much deliberation and formality that slowed the morning's progress. There was a lot of activity around the judges' bench where judges conferred amongst themselves, and the lawyers talked to the judges. I knew I had to be patient, after all I had waited a long time for this day, it may as well not end too soon, I thought.

The next witnesses called by the State were two of Chanal's colleagues from his army days. They had given their statements almost twenty years before, in the mid 80s, when Chanal had first been questioned about the disappearance of conscripts under his command. But in the interim they had not been in touch with Chanal and they had forgotten what they had originally said in their testimony. So when they were each asked the question, 'how hygienic was Pierre Chanal?' they said he was 'meticulous; he would wash and shave very regularly, his room was kept immaculately clean, he was so clean.' The judge asked if he was the sort of man who would pick up a mattress off the ground from the side of the road and put it in his van to sleep on? 'Oh, no,' they answered, 'definitely not.'

Of course, Chanal had claimed that this was exactly what he had done – picked up the mattress from the side of the road, and that this explained where all the hairs had come from. As Nicole translated the soldiers' testimonies, I could feel a huge smile gliding across my face. This is great, I thought, this is really damning to Chanal. If only he were here, I thought. I would love to see his face as he watched his own colleagues condemn him with their praise and loyalty; they were hanging him and they didn't even know it. And pity his poor friends who had no idea how detrimental their testimony would be for Chanal. Oh, to be a fly on the wall of Chanal's hospital room this evening, I mused, when his lawyer recounts the day's events and the evidence of his 'friends'. He will be beside himself with rage. He'll know his goose is cooked and his number's up!

The trial continued until ten o'clock that night. I don't believe the judges even stopped for a glass of water during the day. Nicole worked so hard, translating for fourteen hours straight. She was amazing and I was so grateful to be able to follow every moment of the trial without having to decipher it for myself.

We emerged from the court exhausted. It was dark and there was no one around. Luckily the media had all gone home to their beds and we could make a speedy exit.

We realised then that we hadn't eaten since lunchtime and we were ravenous. Looking around for somewhere to eat, we were lucky to find a little restaurant that was probably the last one still serving in the whole of Reims. We met Patrice Denis's brother, Gil, there too and so asked him to join us for dinner, which he did. We all talked at once and we all talked about the same thing – the day's events. Who had said what, how we felt when we heard Chanal's army buddies talk about him, the various bits of evidence and how it compared with the original statements. We were forensic in our discussion. We had been living, breathing the details of our cases for almost two decades. At last we could talk about them and know, finally, that something real and substantial was being done. I felt for the first time things were going our way, that we were winning. This was everything I had wanted and as I sat and looked at our group, all eyes brimming with emotion as we clinked glasses, I still wanted to pinch myself to make sure it was real.

Meanwhile, a few kilometres away, on the other side of town, Pierre Chanal was resting in his hospital bed. It was 11.30pm. He had just had a visit from his lawyer and had not been at all happy to hear of the day's events. His room was big and the bed was in the middle of the room near two windows, one in front of the bed and one to the side. He was being well cared for. He had doctors and nurses on call. He also had four policemen stationed outside his room, twenty-four hours a day, for his own protection. They had a direct view to his bed where he lay. He could do nothing to harm himself without attracting the guards' attention. If they looked in at him, they saw him lying on his side, with his back to the window.

We finished our meals, tired but exhilarated from our talk and the day's events. We said goodnight to the restaurant owner who was closing up after us, said goodbye to Gil and headed for our comfortable apartment, on loan to us from our generous Irish strangers. It was the perfect end to a successful day. And looking at the cold clear night sky above us, we remarked that tomorrow would be an even better day.

In his hospital room, Chanal's guards looked in on him through the glass in the door. He appeared to be sound asleep. He would probably sleep all night, they thought.

Back in the apartment, Noeleen and I had done enough talking for the day; we could barely look at one another. Judy, James and Tootsie were all shattered. We gave each other a hug before bed. 'Goodnight, sleep well,' I said. 'You too, Mum.' I melted into the warm soft bed, closed my eyes and drifted into the deepest, best sleep ever.

Back in the hospital an alarm was sounding. Police, doctors and nursing staff were rushing in and out of Chanal's room. One of the policemen had noticed a dark liquid pool spreading across the floor under Chanal's bed. He knew there was something seriously wrong.

Chanal had somehow stolen and secreted a portion of an army issue razor blade. He had then cut the top of his jogging pants while lying in his hospital bed. He gathered his sheets in a bundle under his leg to soak up his blood so that he would not attract attention. He used the pants material as a tourniquet and sliced his leg, knowing that the anti-coagulant tablets he was taking for a blood clot would mean that he would bleed very quickly. Within four minutes, he was dead.

We awoke to the sound of the phone ringing. We had not given the number to anyone except *Irish Times* journalist Lara Marlow. 'Something is wrong,' I said, as Noeleen lifted the phone. I could hear Lara's voice but couldn't make out what she was saying. Noeleen repeated her words. Chanal was dead. It was all over. Everything was gone. We turned the television on, hoping it wasn't true. But it was. We both collapsed on the floor and cried, cried so hard. Chanal was dead. It was over, it was finished. Every hope we had was gone with his last breath. He had taken charge in the end; he was in control, in control of the judges, the court, the trial. He had said he wasn't going to go through with it and now he had done it. The bastard. I think I hated him now more then than I had ever done. He robbed me of my son once and now he was robbing me again of any chance of justice. It wasn't damn well fair. It wasn't right.

Hours later we had to get ready and go back to the court so that we could hear officially that Chanal was dead and the trial was collapsed.

Along with the other families, we were taken into a room at the courthouse where the announcement was made officially. We walked into the room shattered and dazed. No one spoke. There were no words for how we felt. Nothing, pure emptiness. The Chief Prosecutor confirmed that Chanal had died. The doctor who had attended Chanal and pronounced him dead was also there and explained how Chanal had died and that it had only taken him approximately four minutes to die. It was then that the quiet of the room was broken. Some families began screaming at the Chief Prosecutor and it looked like they might attack him. He moved towards us and motioned for us to join him in the next room where he explained in English what he had said before.

We couldn't believe that it had been allowed to happen and we believed Chanal must have been in some way facilitated to die. Someone gave him the blade. Someone wasn't doing his or her job properly while Chanal put his endgame in motion.

The Chief Prosecutor told us that there would probably be an investigation and that the whole matter would be dealt with urgently and seriously; answers would be called for.

I demanded that the policemen who let Chanal kill himself be put on trial themselves.

But really there was nothing any of us could do because nothing would bring Chanal back and the trial was over. Chanal's lawyer, Buffard, came over to us. He had approached our lawyer, Cherifa, and asked if he could be introduced to us. This was the first time he had ever spoken to us. He shook hands with me and then with Noeleen, saying he was sorry for what had happened and how it had finished up. His words were nowhere near enough what I needed to hear.

It was to have been day two of the trial and the day I was to give evidence. Instead, I was consoling my kids. They had lost their brother and now they had lost any chance of resolution or justice. Except this time, they couldn't blame me. This time, it wasn't my fault. It didn't make the tragedy any easier.

Among the crowd we caught sight of Palazs Falvay, the young Hungarian boy who had been abducted and raped by Chanal. We had often contemplated going to Hungary to meet with him and Dominique had been in touch with him and he would have come to Paris for a meeting had we pursued it. However, Noeleen and myself talked long and hard about it and decided the boy had been put through enough without having to rake it all up again for our benefit. We decided to leave it.

Palazs Falvay caught my eye and walked over. He had been the only person to survive his ordeal at the hands of Chanal. He was a slight, dark haired young fellow, very serene and calm. He wore spectacles. He gave me the impression of someone who had great religious faith. He didn't talk much except to say that he was glad it was all over, that Chanal was dead. His voice was quiet but measured. As he looked around the room, he said it was better for all the families that Chanal was dead. Finally, he looked straight at me.

'Go home, Madame O'Keeffe,' he said, 'it is better this man is dead. He is in the best place. He should not be on this earth. There are worse things than death.'

The next day, Eric asked us to his office to talk about the case against the French State for the failures in its justice system, for negligence during the sixteen years leading up to the collapse of the trial. The Denis and Gache families were already taking a case. While on the face of it, this was a compensation case for the delays and obstructions that had mired the last sixteen years, it meant that the authorities would have to admit the failings and we we might even get some answers as to why. It was worth doing, but for me, the real battle was over and we had gained nothing short of a hollow victory. Chanal was dead but it wasn't the outcome I wanted. I felt empty and cheated, robbed of a trial. I wanted him to stand trial, I wanted justice. I wanted him to own up to what he did. I know in my heart that he would never have done that voluntarily, but at least in a trial he would have been made to account for Trevor's murder. He would have been convicted, I was sure of it. And best of all, he would have been made to go back to prison, which for him would be worse than death.

Once I signed the documents for the civil case, we packed up to go home. There was nothing to stay for. We would go back to work and wait for the word on the civil case that would take place at the Palais de Justice in Paris. How long would we have to wait on this case?

As we waited for our flight at Charles De Gaulle airport, we reflected on the events of the past few days. How when we got to court, there was actually nothing new in the case. Much of the information and evidence that we finally went to court with was exactly as it had been in the beginning, back in the late 1980s. However we knew that a lot more would have come out during the trial. Even in the one day of the trial we had heard new information, such as the testimony of Chanal's former army colleagues, and more would have come from the recruits who had witnessed firsthand Chanal's behaviour in the army. Noeleen and myself always believed that the case and the evidence from a trial would seriously hurt the army's reputation. When Chanal committed suicide, all this evidence would now be lost forever.

We were given a date for the civil case hearing. We had to have a Paris lawyer with us who would present the evidence to the judges. Eric found us one.

In January 2004, Noeleen finally allowed herself to have her hip replaced. She had always put the operation off because we never knew when we would need to go to trial. There had been times when the pain was so bad, she had not been able to walk, and I remember one time in 2000 having to leave her leaning on a window sill in Lille while I went off to find a hotel. Her hip had locked and she was completely immobilised.

Even now, Noeleen postponed her second hip operation in order to go to France and was only finally able to go through with the operation in 2005.

We were invited to the hearing towards the end of November 2004. Inside the courtroom there were three judges presiding over the case. We weren't the only family there. In all, there were forty plaintiffs from all the families of Chanal's victims, who had joined the lawsuit against the State. With us were Eric and Helena Bolstein, our new Paris lawyer. Helena was about to present the evidence when an almighty argument broke out between Eric and the judges. From what we could gather, the judges had not received what they believed to be the requisite paperwork from Saint-Quentin, in particular they needed more files from Judge Marien, the original investigating magistrate. Eric argued that the file ran to 100 volumes, that the court would never be able to get through it. He said it had been Judge Marien who had sat on the case for five years and done nothing to move it on, that all the evidence had been present in 1989 but that Pierre Chanal was not investigated for Trevor's murder until 1994, and even then, Judge Marien ruled the evidence was insufficient to charge Chanal. He argued that the evidence available in 1998 was the same evidence that was used to charge Chanal in 2001. I had never seen Eric so angry. He got up out of his seat and went right up to the judges' bench and screamed into their faces. We couldn't catch exactly what he was saying but it was obvious to everyone that he was not happy. At one point it looked like he was going to be thrown out of the courtroom. The president of the judges told Eric to save his performance for another court! A guard appeared from another room and hovered until the voices of Eric and the judges calmed down somewhat. He then discreetly left the court, but as soon as Eric's voice was raised again, he came back in. I was sure he would be arrested. At the end of the morning, Eric agreed to come back to the court in January 2005.

About five weeks later, we heard that the judges had reached a decision and we were given the day, time and place when the ruling would be handed down. The time fixed was 2pm but Noeleen and I liked to be on time, so we arrived an hour or so early at the Palais de Justice. We met Lara Marlow in a little coffee shop opposite the building. Lara was covering the story for *The Irish Times* and by this stage we trusted her completely. We ordered coffee and sat down, though always keeping an eye on the time. Our Paris lawyer, Helena, arrived soon after and joined us. At half past one, Noeleen and I got up to leave; we would go across the road and find our courtroom ahead of the two o'clock deadline. Lara and Helena followed us out. There was a queue of people waiting to go in to the courtrooms and bags had to be searched and documents checked. The security people were brisk and we didn't have to wait too long before we were inside and walking up the grand steps to the main foyer. We checked the name and number of the courtroom that we had to go to. However, when we got there we discovered that the ruling had already been handed down. We had missed it. Journalists waiting outside the courtroom had received the ruling from a court attendant, not at two o'clock as expected, but an hour earlier. So, while we were sitting in the coffee shop opposite, watching the time so as not to be late, the case was actually being dealt with in our absence. The journalists handed us the ruling. It said that 'Serious misconduct was noted. The State was responsible, so the State must pay damages.' An award of €25,000 would be paid out to each member of the families.

Although the ruling was welcome, the way in which it had been handled and delivered seemed highly irregular. But Noeleen and I were not surprised. 'When have we ever had a straight deal with the French law system?' we remarked. The answer was 'never'. Noeleen reckoned it was because the judges did not want the decision to be made in the public glare of journalists. However, the decision of the judges was unprecedented in French law in that they acknowledged that the case had been badly handled. They admitted they had made a mistake. Eric said that this was the first time ever in the history of the State that they had admitted and apologised for the wrongdoing and inadequacy of the justice system. Years later, Lara Marlowe told us that the ruling had been one of the highlights of her year.

For the other families it was a momentous decision because it was the first time there was formal and public acknowledgement that their boys were dead and had actually been killed by Chanal; that they had not deserted or disappeared voluntarily.

I struggled to take comfort from the ruling. For me, it was always about getting justice for Trevor, at any cost. And the cost, the personal cost to my family and me, had been enormous. Even after eighteen years, my family could not talk about Trevor without tears. Recently my son James came to me to confess that he believed Trevor's death was his fault. He told me his story. Sometime after Trevor began working in St Alban's he had rung James and asked, 'Can I come down to London and work with you?' At the time, James was running a successful rickshaw in London's Chinatown. 'No,' James responded. 'I'm not carrying you around all day when I could be making money.' 'OK then,' said Trevor defiantly, 'I'll go to France.' That had been the last James heard of Trevor, until we were told that his body had been found in a field in France. I put my arms around him. It broke my heart to think that James had carried this piercing guilt all these years. I too carried the same guilt, blaming myself for Trevor's death. After all, what sort of a mother loses her child? I had lost my child and spent the next decade and a half trying to protect the remaining four. Yet at the heart of it all I knew that there was only ever one person who was responsible for Trevor's death, and that was Pierre Chanal, the man who killed him. And when he died, that, to me, was the end of it, for my family and me.

Not long afterwards, Noeleen received some information from her lawyer about Caroline's case. There had been a new development. The investigating magistrate had finally made an announcement on the case, saying that no proper police investigation had been carried out in the aftermath of Caroline's death. An autopsy that should have been carried out had not been carried out and the scene of her death had not been preserved. Caroline and Trevor's circumstances were eerily similar. The crucial first hours and days after their deaths had not been properly policed. For Noeleen and I, inadequate policing would mean that ultimately the chances of finding our children's murderers would be all the more difficult, if not impossible.

Eric is keen to pursue a further case against the French State for their reponsibility in allowing Chanal to commit suicide while in their care, and I'll do what I have to, turn up for court when I'm needed. In some ways I'm glad it's at an end. Of course, I would prefer that Chanal was still alive but rotting in jail. There are worse things than death, after all. But I know I have to move on. I'm just not sure how to go about it.

I called Eric recently and he signed off by saying, 'Now, Eroline, you can call me again in a month's time.' 'A month?' I laughed, 'I've never waited a month to call you.' But I'm actually going to call him this week, because that will be two weeks since I spoke to him and it feels like a month.

I find myself trying to persuade Noeleen to pursue her case for Caroline. Her case is closed at the moment but it could be opened tomorrow if the right bit of evidence could be unearthed, or the right person came forward with a crucial piece of information. 'We could go to France and look for clues; we only need one small breakthrough to get started,' I encourage her. 'I would be there for you the way you've been there for me.'

She said she's thinking about it.

Chronology of Events 1977-1990

1977-1986: Pierre Chanal serves in the 4th dragoon regiment at Mourmelon

4 January 1980: Patrick Dubois, of the 4th tank regiment at Mourmelon, disappears. Desertion proceedings are begun.

20 February 1981: Serge Havel, of the 3rd artillery regiment at Mailly, disappears after getting leave to visit his family.

7 August 1981: Manuel Carvalho of the 4th dragoon regiment at Mourmelon goes on weekend leave and disappears.

20 August 1981: Pascal Sargent of the 503rd tank regiment at Mourmelon does not return from leave.

30 September 1982: Olivier Donner of the 503rd tank regiment at Mourmelon disappears.

31 October 1982: Body of Olivier Donner found. A judicial investigation begins at Troyes. The existence of a serial killer in the area begins to be suspected.

2 August 1984: With no more disappearances recorded, the files on Dubois, Havel, Sargent and Donner are closed

23 August 1985: Patrice Denis, a civilian who was going to the camp at Mourmelon disappears.

27 August 1985: Judicial enquiry into the 'abduction' of Patrice Denis opens in Chalons-en-Champagne.

August 1986: Pierre Chanal is transferred to Fontainebleau.

30 April 1987: Patrick Gache of the 4th dragoon regiment at Mourmelon leaves the camp and fails to return.

8 August 1987: Discovery of the body of Trevor O'Keeffe at Alaincourt in l'Aisne.

9 August 1988: Arrest near Macon of Pierre Chanal, who was found with a Hungarian hitchiker, Palazs Falvay, in his Volkswagen van. The young man had been sexually assaulted.

23 October 1990:The Court of Assizes of Saone-et-Loire sentences Pierre Chanal to ten years in prison for rape, indecent assault and abduction of Palazs Falvay.

More information on the 'Disappeared of Mourmelon' can be found on
www.disparusdemourmelon.org

OTHER BOOKS FROM
THE O'BRIEN PRESS

AFRAID OF THE DARK
The Tragic Story of Robert Holohan
Ralph Riegel

For eight days in 2005 the nation was transfixed by the disappearance of eleven-year-old Robert Holohan. Hope turned to horror when his body was found and his killer was revealed as his good friend and neighbour.

Ralph Riegel covered the tragedy as it unfolded, from the search through the court case and the DPP appeal. He reveals the pain of the local community, the dedication of searchers and organisers, and the aftereffects of Majella Holohan's astonishing Victim Impact Statement.

DEATH IN DECEMBER
The Story of Sophie Toscan du Plantier
Michael Sheridan

On 23 December 1996, the body of Sophie Toscan du Plantier was discovered outside her remote holiday cottage near Schull in West Cork. The murder caused shock waves in her native France and in the quiet Cork countryside that she had chosen as her retreat from the film business in which she and her husband mixed. Despite an extensive investigation, the killer is still at large.

Seven years after Sophie's brutal death, an extraordinary libel hearing revealed new details of the events surrounding the murder. Journalist Ralph Riegel gives a day-by-day account of what one barrister described as 'the Irish libel case of the century'.

LIFE SENTENCE
Murder Victims and their Families
Catherine Cleary

Death in any circumstances is devastating, but when the cause is murder, grief takes on an extra dimension. Those left behind live under a life sentence, condemned to years of painful memories and deep regrets.

Based on personal interviews with victims' families, Catherine Cleary tells the horrific stories of twelve murders and how their families survived the ordeal.

Send for our full-colour catalogue